The
Overcomers

The Overcomers

RUSSELL CHANDLER

Fleming H. Revell Company
Old Tappan, New Jersey

Scripture references identified KJV are from the King James Version of the Bible.

Scripture quotations identified RSV are from the Revised Standard Version of the Bible, copyrighted 1946, 1952, © 1971 and 1973.

Scripture quotations identified LB are from The Living Bible, Copyright © 1971 by Tyndale House Publishers, Wheaton, Illinois 60187. All rights reserved.

Scripture quotations identified PHILLIPS are from THE NEW TESTAMENT IN MODERN ENGLISH (Revised Edition), translated by J. B. Phillips. Copyright © J. B. Phillips, 1958, 1960, 1972. Used by permission of Macmillan Publishing Co., Inc.

Excerpts from "Christian Education Trends" by Paul S. Rees are reprinted by permission of World Vision magazine, April 1977.

The poem "Impossible means that i" is used by permission from I Love the Word Impossible by Ann Kiemel, © 1976 by Tyndale House Publishers, Inc., Wheaton, Illinois.

The poem "For You It Might Have Been an Easy Decision" by Ann Kiemel is from I'm Out to Change My World, copyright © 1974 by Impact Books, a Division of the Benson Company. Used by permission.

Photo of Vonette Bright by Earhart Photography.

Library of Congress Cataloging in Publication Data

Chandler, Russell.
    The overcomers.

    CONTENTS: His will brings her joy: Elisabeth Elliot.—Towering theologian: Carl F. Henry.—They just praise the Lord: Bill and Gloria Gaither.—Hang in there, brother: E. V. Hill.—Woman of prayer: Vonette Bright. [etc.]
      1. Christian biography. 2. Christian life—1960– I. Title.
BR1700.2.C46   209'.2'2   78-16621
ISBN 0-8007-0944-6

Contents

5

      Maria Von Trapp   89

8   Thoughtful Quaker
      D. Elton Trueblood   97

9   He Tries God
      Walter Hoving   107

10   Pastoral Partners
      Frederick W. and Ruth P. Cropp   118

11   Southern Singer
      Joanne Cash Yates   131

12   Elder Statesman
      Paul S. Rees   144

      Conclusion:
      Through It All . . .   155

Introduction

One clear evening in the spring of 1977, Ernie Owen and Dick Baltzell of the Fleming H. Revell Company and I sat down in the Velvet Turtle Restaurant in Los Angeles to discuss book possibilities. I had just read a report in the April issue of *Redbook* magazine. It said that 90 percent of women surveyed believed that God had helped them through specific critical situations in life. And an overwhelming majority said they had felt God's presence in a special way through a born-again experience similar to that described by President Jimmy Carter about himself.

With such an interest in personal religion, why do so many people still seem to be floundering? And if, on the other hand, so many do feel God's guiding hand can help them in crises, wouldn't it be a blessing for well-known Christians who have found spiritual sufficiency in Jesus Christ to share their insights with others?

Ernie and Dick liked the idea. Out of our conversations came the framework for *The Overcomers*.

The book, we decided, would present testimonies of specific spiritual help experienced by evangelical Christian personalities, most of them quite well known. The persons would be young and old, men and women, and of different races and backgrounds. The main theme would go beyond merely recounting their life stories or conversion experiences.

What was needed, I thought, was to explore how Christians can face crises victoriously, as well as cope with the daily hangnail irritations of life.

Where *can* we turn for spiritual help in times of disappointment, struggle, and testing?

In the process of interviewing these fourteen noted Christians (five men, five women, and two couples), I found out. It lifted my faith to learn how they overcame. And I grew excited about passing along spiritual truths and practical lessons to you through their book. For it is, after all, far more *their* book than it is mine.

The Overcomers digs deeper than telling how they did it. It tells how *they* do it—and how you can, too, through the Spirit of Christ. *The Overcomers* is relational, based on the proven experiences of some great Christians, who, despite their well-known successes and stature, are nevertheless not that much different from you and me.

This book is for all Christians, especially new ones, struggling ones, tired ones, and mediocre ones. It is also for people who think there just might be something worth exploring in the Christian faith—that Jesus Christ, just maybe, could make a difference and bring an abundant life.

I conducted interviews throughout the country, mostly in the summer of 1977, with these gracious men and women. Here are the questions I asked:

1. Once you became a Christian, what was the most trying or difficult time or event(s) in your life?

2. Where did you turn for help? Who helped you? How? What did you read? Did you pray? Did it help?

3. What do you do now about recurring doubts, anxieties, or disappointments? In other words, how do you get the victory when things seem to be going wrong?

4. What lifts you out of daily anxiety?

5. How do you plug into these resources?

6. How would the spiritual lessons you have learned benefit others? Would they have to have the same problems you did to be helped?

7. Can a Christian be sitting on top of the world all the time? Should he or she try to?

Actually, most interviews went far beyond the suggested questions. We came to grips with the kinds of problems all humans face and from which Christians are not exempt: worry, health, aging, death, vocations, money, sex, marriage and divorce, identity and self-actualization, child rearing, and success and failure.

The concluding chapter draws together common threads from the interviews and shows how the Word and Holy Spirit can link God's help to human hurts. It incorporates some of my own views and interpretations about how Christians can overcome. The writing has been fun—not only because the project came at a significant crossroads in my own life, but also because interpretation and a little editorializing are delicious morsels not often savored by a straight reporter who writes news of religion for a large metropolitan newspaper.

A very special thanks to Marjorie Lee Lund, an accomplished writer, a constant source of encouragement and inspiration, who typed and checked the manuscript.

RUSSELL CHANDLER

Psalms 32:8

The
Overcomers

Elisabeth Elliot

1

His Will Brings Her Joy

"The glory of God's will for us means absolute trust. It means the will to do His will, and it means joy."

With these words, Elisabeth Elliot, the famed American missionary whose husband was speared to death while taking the Gospel to the Stone Age tribe of Auca Indians in South America, began a major address at the 1976 Urbana convention.

"The Apostle Paul was absolutely sure of his Master," she continued, speaking to a crowd of 17,000—mostly students, 700 missionaries, and a sprinkling of pastors—who had given up part of their Christmas vacation to flock to the little prairie town in southern Illinois to hear the commands of Christ for evangelism, discipleship, and missions. Elisabeth, wearing a long-sleeved full-length dress, smiled as she stood behind a battery of microphones on the podium. The name, Inter-Varsity Christian Fellowship, sponsor of the triennial Urbana conventions since 1947, was emblazoned diagonally across the side of the speaker's stand.

"Paul never said, 'I know why this is happening.' He said, 'I know *whom* I have believed. I am absolutely sure that nothing can separate us from the love of God,' " Elisabeth told the attentive audience jamming the huge assembly hall on the campus of the University of Illinois.

Her message was forged in the fire of personal experience.

Much of that experience is told in her eleven books, which include the well-known *Shadow of the Almighty* and *Through Gates of Splendor.*

Other details of the glory and the cost of following God's will were poured out later by the purposeful and twice-widowed Bible translator and theology teacher during a summer interview.

Born in Brussels, Belgium, of missionary parents (her father also was editor of the *Sunday School Times* in Philadelphia), Elisabeth majored in classical Greek at Wheaton College. There she faced the first serious test of her faith. It came in the form of a man who later was to become her husband. The test was her love life.

CAREER CHOICE

"When I was a senior in college," she related, "I believed God was taking me through a period of *exercise of the soul* in order to be willing to go to the mission field as a single woman. I had told God that I was willing to be a missionary, but that I was not really willing to be single for the rest of my life."

She knew that chances of finding a husband in the mission field were slight, and it was considerable time before she was able to surrender the matter to the Lord.

Soon after saying Yes, Lord, to being single, Elisabeth found herself in love with a student named Jim Elliot. To add to the predicament, and to her utter astonishment, the week before graduation at Wheaton Jim confessed his feelings for her. Worse, from the human point of view,

Jim also confessed that God had taken him through exactly the same period of testing. He had come to the place where he was willing to go to the mission field as a single man, following the steps of the Apostle Paul.

"As far as we knew at that point," Elisabeth remembers, "that was that."

How God led the two of them from that point on is detailed in her book, *Shadow of the Almighty*, essentially a biography of Jim.

"It is logical that God tests those who would follow Him most severely and painfully at the point of their love life," Elisabeth commented.

That is one of the most acute issues in the life of a young person—and those not so young, too.

"If we are followers of the Crucified," observed Elisabeth, "it stands to reason that we will encounter the Cross. And, where would we expect that Cross to be presented to us? Is it not at the point of deepest need or deepest feeling?"

For Elisabeth and Jim that was the case; it was her first trying and difficult time. It lasted for five years. Not until then did God give any clear direction that they were to be married.

"We were both single missionaries in Ecuador, on different sides of the Andes, where communication was erratic, to say the least. It could easily take six weeks to write a letter and receive an answer from the other side of the mountain.

"So," reflected Elisabeth, "there were many lessons in loneliness, patience, and self-restraint—and waiting on God—because of our love for each other."

SEVERE TRIALS

Asked to recall other trying or difficult events in her life, Elisabeth, who first went to South America to do translation work in 1952, mentioned three experiences of loss in that first year working with a small tribe of Indians called the Colorados in the western jungles of Ecuador. Elisabeth, then single, was reducing the Colorados' language to writing.

The first calamity was the murder of the informant who was giving her information about the language and culture of the Colorados. There was no one to take his place.

A second catastrophe was the loss of all the work Elisabeth did that year. All her files, tapes, notebooks, and vocabulary compilations were stolen, and no copies or duplicates existed.

The same year, Jim was reconstructing a small jungle mission station among the Quichua Indians. During a sudden flood one night, all of the buildings he had rebuilt plus three new ones were swept away down the Amazon River.

These three experiences of total earthly loss taught Elisabeth and Jim the deep lessons that Jesus taught His disciples: "Truly, truly I say unto you, unless a grain of wheat falls into the earth and dies, it remains alone; but if it dies, it bears much fruit" (John 12:24 RSV).

The practical outcome of that lesson was this, according to Elisabeth: "I had to face up to the fact in those stunning losses that God was indeed sovereign; therefore, He was my Lord, my Master, the One in charge of my life, the One who deserved my worship and my service. The road to eternal gain leads inevitably through earthly loss. True faith is operative in the dark. True faith deals with the inexplicable things of life. If we have explanations—if things are clear and simple—there's not very much need for faith.

"Through these three experiences of loss before either of us had been a jungle missionary for a full year, we came to know Jesus Christ in a deeper way and to begin to enter into the lessons that Paul describes in Philippians: 'But whatever gain I had, I counted as loss for the sake of

Christ. Indeed I count everything as loss because of the surpassing worth of knowing Christ Jesus my Lord . . .' " (3:7, 8 RSV).

Elisabeth clung to those verses, and several other favorites, during that first year and at other crises in her life.

In particular, the Lord helped her in 1956 when she had been married only three years and had an infant daughter Valerie. That was when Jim and four American missionary companions were massacred by the Aucas.

The promise that God gave her that first year is in Isaiah 50:7 RSV: "For the Lord God helps me; therefore I have not been confounded; therefore I have set my face like a flint, and I know that I shall not be put to shame."

Elisabeth does not spurn human counselors during times of trouble. Many are willing to hear out recounting of the troubles of most people today, she feels. But in her case, she was more or less alone. During the eleven years she was a missionary in Ecuador, seldom was anyone near at hand to whom she could turn. Even other missionaries had their hands full ministering to the Indians without having to minister to an anxious, suffering missionary. So Elisabeth learned to turn to the Lord directly, and to His Word, for her consolation and stability, rather than to cry on other people's shoulders.

God's comfort was sufficient.

SOURCES OF STRENGTH

Elisabeth has always turned also to reading material as a source of strength and guidance. The Bible, of course, is basic. She reads it regularly, studies it, underlines it, and makes notes in the margin and in her own notebook. The *Daily Light,* a small devotional book of pure Scripture, has been of help to Elisabeth, as it has to many, and she reads it every day. Great missionary books are on her list. She singled out works by such greats as Amy Carmichael of India, whom she calls perhaps the greatest influence on her life of any single writer. She has read the biographies of Hudson Taylor, David Brainerd, James Frazer, Mary Slessor, and others. Devotional favorites include Thomas à Kempis's *The Imitation of Christ,* and Brother Lawrence's *Practice of the Presence of God.*

Prayer? "Of course," she replied. "I prayed very often with almost no faith at all—probably faith much smaller than a grain of mustard seed" (*see* Matthew 13:31–32). Yet, according to Jesus' parable, that minute seed produced a mighty shrub, large enough to accommodate birds and their nests.

The visible results of prayer are not that easily discernible in human terms, Elisabeth feels, because prayer is not subject to the kind of measurement one can project from a seed to a tree. To her, prayer is a force, like gravity, that God has built into the universe and with which we must cooperate. Equally powerful and inevitable, prayer is a spiritual, rather than a physical, force. It is one way God allows us to cooperate with Him. But the results must be left in His hands.

Elisabeth is convinced God would not have commanded His people to pray if it were a useless activity. To illustrate her point, she cited Revelation 8:3, which gives a picture of an angel with a golden censer who offers up prayers of the saints along with the smoke of incense to God.

"That seems to be an indication that no prayer to God is ever lost," she said. "Just exactly what forces are set in motion when a human being prays is a mystery. And yet, God is accomplishing His purposes. There was never any doubt at all in my mind, in the midst of these losses—the death of my informant, the theft of my materials, the destruction by flood of the station where Jim had been working—there was no question that God was sovereign, that He was in charge, and that He would ultimately give to Himself glory, because of these things.

"And yet, the experience of loss is inevitably painful. We are human beings. We suffer. The Scripture makes it clear, from beginning to end, that there is no glory without suffering, no gain without loss, no joy without sorrow. These are all the paradoxes of Christianity. The Cross is a symbol of suffering and a symbol of glory. The Cross doesn't exempt us from human woes, but transforms these woes. That is the secret of Christian faith— the transformation of sin and suffering and evil."

DOUBTS, ANXIETIES, DISAPPOINTMENTS

Turning to the area of doubts, anxieties, and disappointments, Elisabeth paused for a moment, then admitted that every day something comes up that puts her right back in the kindergarten of faith. That seemed like quite an admission from one known for the sturdy quality of her commitment, faith, and endurance.

Elisabeth went on to explain by asking a series of rhetorical questions: "Do you believe God loves you? Can you trust Him for this thing? Will you rest in His promises? Is He in charge? In other words, how do you get the victory when things seem to be going wrong?

"To answer that question simply would make it look as if this was 'Elliot gets the victory' immediately and continually as she needs it. This would be very far from the truth."

Elisabeth recalled that her grandfather used to have a motto over his desk that read, "Not somehow, but triumphantly."

"My motto," she confided, "if I were to be truthful, would have to be 'Not triumphantly, but somehow.' " But she added: "Yet I know, beyond any shadow of doubt, that the only victory that overcomes the world is faith. I don't look at the data of my life and deduce that God is benevolent, loving, and kind from that data. In fact, there are data which a skeptic would interpret as a stunning array of evidence that God does *not* care, that He is *not* sovereign, that He is *not* loving—perhaps that He is *not* even there."

How, then, does she look at the evidence and still believe the love of God and His sovereign purpose? By faith. Belief. "I really believe with my whole heart that all things do, in fact, fit into a pattern for good. As the J. B. Phillips translation of Romans 8:28 puts it: 'Moreover we know that to those who love God, who are called according to his plan, everything that happens fits into a pattern for good.' "

Though some may think of Elisabeth, who lived and worked with the Aucas in a jungle clearing for two years, as some sort of supersaint, she is quick to admit that she, too, is subject to anxieties and moods. Yet the promises of God lift her out of such times: "Because He lives, I can face tomorrow," she said, quoting a line from one of the best-known Gaither hymns.

In answering my next question, Elisabeth made it clear she didn't like the phrasing of it. "How do you plug into the resources of God to overcome anxieties?" I had asked. To her, it sounded too much like some technique.

"A Christian doesn't 'plug into' God," she explained. "A Christian surrenders to God. He chooses the course which is the will of God. He doesn't simply add the will of God to his own plans and purposes. He surrenders them."

SURRENDER

Elisabeth finds help in surrendering her plans to God through repeating the prayer of another great missionary—Betty Scott. She and her husband, missionaries to China, were beheaded in the 1930s. Elisabeth Elliot first prayed that prayer when she was eleven years old. Later, she copied it into her Bible when she was a teenager. She quoted it from memory:

"Lord, I give up all of my own plans and purposes, all my desires and hopes. I accept Thy will for my life. I give myself, my life, my all, utterly to Thee, to be Thine forever. Fill me. Conceal me with Thy Holy Spirit. Use me as Thou wilt. Send me where Thou wilt. Work out Thy whole will in my life at any cost—now and forever."

That dedication took Elisabeth Elliot from the Auca work back to language and Bible translation with the Quichua Indians in 1961 and to the United States in 1963. Three years later she married Addison H. Leitch, a theologian and professor, who died in 1973. The following year, Elisabeth became visiting professor at Gordon-Conwell Theological Seminary in Wenham, Massachusetts.

About the same time, two seminary men from Gordon-Conwell came to Elisabeth's house in Hamilton as boarders, both of them tall, blond, blue-eyed southerners. Walt Shephard, Jr., and Lars Gren stayed with Elisabeth for two of their three seminary years.

"I found Lars a most thoughtful, tactful, helpful, pleasant, and amusing lodger," Elisabeth said, "but after he graduated I began to see him with eyes other than a landlady's."

On December 21, 1977, Lars and Elisabeth celebrated her fifty-first birthday, Christmas, and their marriage in Christ Church in Hamilton. Meanwhile, Walt Shephard had married Elisabeth's daughter, Valerie!

Elisabeth described her wedding to Lars: "The ceremony, from the Prayer Book of 1662 (with bits about procreation deleted), was very brief, followed by a reception given by the women of a little Bible class I've been teaching. We had three nights in the Parker House in Boston and then returned to Hamilton for Christmas with Walt, Val, and little seven-month-old Walter III."

After the holidays, Elisabeth and Lars moved to Smyrna, Georgia, a suburb of Atlanta, so Lars could complete a hospital chaplaincy internship at a state hospital in the area.

Through the years, one of the greatest encouragements in Elisabeth's spiritual life—in overcoming—has been the testimony of other believers. She points to that testimony in the Scriptures as well, particularly Hebrews 12:1 RSV where the writer says, "Therefore, since we are surrounded by so great a cloud of witnesses . . . ." Elisabeth reminded me that the writer has just cited in the eleventh chapter all the people from Noah right down to the people who were sawn in two.

"I recognize that the race that is set before me is not the same as somebody else's," she said, "but for another person to know that God is faithful to me in every crisis of my life—in every moment of every day—is to know that it is the same God who loves everybody else. So spiritual lessons that I have learned surely can benefit others if they will trust that same God."

To be helped, she added, others don't need to have had experiences similar to hers. In fact, she sees herself sometimes at a disadvantage in this respect because her life has been unusual, if not exotic, in many ways.

"I always try to point out that it is the same Lord who chooses the arena in which we are to run our own race. He is the one who chooses the set of circumstances in which we are appointed to glorify Him," she declared. "So, the God of Abraham, Isaac, and Jacob, and the God of Paul and Silas, and Amy Carmichael, James Frazer, Hudson Taylor, and Elisabeth Elliot is the same God who is available to everyone. I know that He is totally trustworthy."

Commenting on the fact that she had lost two husbands, Elisabeth suggested that her experience—though similar—would not exactly match that of others who have been widowed. Each widow will respond, in some measure, in light of who she is, who her husband was, and what the circumstances of the death were.

"It is comforting to me to realize," Elisabeth elaborated, "that it is not the experiences of our lives which change us, but it is our *response* to those experiences. After all, the children of Israel, wandering in the wilderness, all had the same experience. But some responded with faith and others responded with rebellion. We have exactly the same choice today.

"There are people who go through indescribably horrible circumstances who come out as refined gold. Others go through lesser trials and are embittered. Why? Because their response is rebellion—defiance of God rather than obedience. Everything you do is swelling the chorus of praise—or swelling the shout of defiance against God."

NOT ALWAYS ON TOP OF THINGS

Can a Christian feel on top of things all the time, then? "Emphatically not," asserts Elisabeth.

"We need only to read the Psalms to realize there is such a thing as miry clay, the pit out of which the psalmist himself describes his deliverance. Many of the psalms are moans and wails to God: 'How long, Lord? Why are You doing this to me? Why don't You listen? Where are You?'

"Paul himself describes anxiety and fear. Jesus was delivered from His fear when He prayed in the Garden of Gethsemane. We are subject to all kinds of emotions and temptations. So I think it is a very cruel distortion of Christianity to advertise nothing but happiness all the time—'wonderful peace of mind since I found the Lord,' plink-a-plink-a-plink—that kind of thing. It is a hideous distortion of the Gospel, which deals with suffering. The victory over that kind of suffering can be won only by faith, not by feelings."

Elisabeth believes that the present age is one in which feelings are given priority. But nothing, she says, can be more misleading or destructive, because a person's feelings are so ephemeral. As soon as they sink, a person who bases his faith on them will be immediately shaken. That kind of faith will collapse very quickly under the pressure of life.

Elisabeth says, "I have to operate without reference to my feelings. It doesn't really matter how I feel about a thing, my responsibility is to be obedient. I need not wait until I feel like obeying."

The case of Ezekiel illustrates the need to obey, she noted. In Ezekiel 24:18 (KJV) the prophet tells about the death of his wife, which God had told him to prepare for: "So I spake unto the people in the morning: and at even my wife died; and I did in the next morning as I was commanded."

"This," Elisabeth said confidently, "is the victory that overcomes the world, through faith. Paul said, '. . . I know whom I have believed, and am persuaded that he is able to keep that which I have committed unto him against that day' (2 Timothy 1:12 KJV). Regardless of my feelings I am to be obedient and to walk in faith, recognizing that seldom will I feel spiritual about it. But I don't have to feel ethereal or pious or holy to present my body daily to God.

"I offer up to Him in prayer my time, my energy, my talents, my work, my money, my reputation, my body, all that I am and have. That is an act of spiritual worship. And I have to believe that God accepts that."

WITH THANKSGIVING

Elisabeth closed the interview by singling out something not previously mentioned but terribly important: thanksgiving.

"If I really believe that God loves me," she said, "if on the evidence of the whole Bible and all those Christians whose lives I've read about, and those whose lives I've personally observed, I can see that He's a faithful God, then surely there is infinite cause for thanksgiving.

"Nothing could be a more effective balance wheel to my life than the giving of thanks. And I believe a strange transformation takes place in the way I see things—in the circumstances themselves—when I give thanks."

In clarification, Elisabeth interjected that she does not see in Scripture a command to give thanks *for* everything. If so, that would mean that we should thank God for evil, sin, and suffering of every kind.

Though Elisabeth cannot imagine thanking God for evil, yet she does thank Him in the midst of whatever circumstances come her way.

"To see my first husband murdered and to see my second husband disintegrate with cancer were things for which I could hardly give thanks. But they were circumstances in which I was absolutely convinced that God was in charge. And therefore, I was able to give thanks, because He was ultimately working out His purposes."

During those experiences, she is certain, God gave her opportunity to comprehend His plan in ways that otherwise would not have been possible.

The congregation of the church Elisabeth attended in Massachusetts affirms together three tremendous statements: Christ has died. Christ has risen. Christ will come again.

"I hang my soul on those strong pegs," she said resolutely, realizing that nothing that happens today, nothing that has happened, nothing that can possibly happen, can ever change in the smallest detail those tremendous facts.

"That is the ground, the bedrock, of my faith. My faith rests there—on the death, Resurrection, and coming again of Christ—not on my own notion or blueprint of how my life is supposed to work. Not on my own feelings. Not on my own spirituality. But on Jesus Christ Himself."

Carl F. H. Henry

2

Towering Theologian

Carl Ferdinand Howard Henry learned to type when he was a student at Islip (Long Island) High School in New York State.

That, he says, is near the top of the list of the important skills he has acquired in life.

For, from early days, when he became a newspaper reporter and editor, to important posts in theological seminaries, to the editorship of an influential Christian magazine, Carl Henry has tapped out some of the most significant articles, books—even tomes—of evangelical theology in this century.

The American Baptist minister is generally acknowledged to be the most noted evangelical theologian in the United States. Before he was sixty-five, Henry had written more than two dozen books, edited nine others, and for twelve years was founding editor of the national journal of evangelical news and thought, *Christianity Today*.

This is the era of the evangelical. Bible-believing Christians have emerged from the subculture into today's cultural limelight. Henry estimates their number at about 50 million, scattered both inside and outside of all of the religious denominations.

"Evangelicals have come out of the cellar coal bins, onto the front porches, and into the main streets of America," he observes.

Henry would be too modest to add that no small measure of the current visibility and respectability of evangelicalism can be traced to his influence—and his prolific pen.

And his typewriter keys keep flying as he continues to work on volumes three and four of his four-volume magnum opus, *God, Revelation & Authority*. The religion news editor of the *New York Times* has called the first two volumes, published in 1976, "the most important work of evangelical theology in recent times."

The intellectual challenge of lecturing and writing, and the satisfaction of seeing the widespread acceptance of works like *God, Revelation & Authority* delight the tall, bespectacled theologian-strategist, who lives in Arlington, Virginia, with his wife, Helga.

But, he said during a series of interviews on the sundeck of his attractive split-level hillside home, he has had many rewarding experiences since he first became a Christian in Long Island.

It was then that he thrust aside everything, including a promising newspaper career, to enroll in a Christian liberal arts school, Wheaton College in Illinois.

"As the oldest of eight children in a poor immigrant family I learned self-reliance at an early age," he recalled.

"But self-reliance will not qualify one for the Kingdom of God. Moral and spiritual vitality came only when the Risen Christ regenerated me at the outset of my journalistic career. I have learned that only a perpetually renewed infilling of the Holy Spirit thwarts the ever-reasserting old self, and imparts the virtues that mold us in the image of Christ.

"There is nothing in this world we can happily take with us into the world to come—nothing at all except what God has given us: a life created in His image, its sins graciously forgiven, its joys hopefully centered in Christ, and its future brightened by the prospect of the glorious presence of God."

Though that glorious presence of God had been patently real to young Henry, the only one in his family to attend college, as he set off for Wheaton, he soon ran head-on into something totally unexpected.

The episode may sound like something less than shattering. Still, Henry lists it as one of three or four of the most trying or difficult times in his growth and development as a Christian.

"God had promised me when I spent half a night on my knees in prayer in Long Island that He would financially see me through college to prepare me for Christian service. I wrote on a three-by-five card the ways that God would meet my college costs: teaching, typing, and newspaper reporting."

By pounding the streets Henry landed a part-time job stringing for the *Wheaton Daily Journal* and the *Chicago Tribune*. The college news bureau had hired a secular journalist to get press visibility for the school. And that journalist and Henry soon crossed pens.

"I apparently angered him," Henry remembers, "by certain articles that I wrote personally and for which I was reimbursed by these papers. He circulated the report that 'Henry claims to be a newspaper reporter, but he's had no journalistic experience whatsoever.' "

I WAS CRUSHED

"I was crushed," Henry recalls painfully, "that I should run into that kind of thing on a Christian campus."

Henry's credentials included working his way up to becoming the youngest editor of the *Smithtown Star*, a weekly paper in the Long Island suburbs, and serving as a correspondent for several large dailies, including the old *New York Herald Tribune*, the *New York Daily News* and the *New York Times*. He had high prospects of a rewarding journalistic career before ever going to college!

Henry spent a sleepless night after the run-in with the other Wheaton reporter.

"I had romanticized a Christian college campus," Henry remarked, noting that this can be a pitfall for many a young, idealistic Christian student. "To have to cope with a member of the staff who dismissed me as a nobody in the area of my own special competence was a totally baffling turn of things."

But the last turn of events wasn't in yet. Through Henry's roommate, the school's dean heard about the problem, called Henry in and reached an agreement whereby stories about the college were to emanate only from the campus news bureau. In turn, the bureau would transmit releases for Henry's string of papers through him.

"God providentially turned this into a situation in which the newspapers reimbursed me when they used material that the news bureau prepared," Henry declared. "I had prayed with my roommate. I had confidence that God had the future in His hands. The outcome reminded me of Romans 8:28 (LB): 'And we know that all that happens to us is working for our good if we love God and are fitting into his plans.' "

A later twist—a further turning of the tables—brought added satisfaction to Henry: He subsequently was asked and agreed to teach journalism at Wheaton.

The second trying, but faith-strengthening, episode

singled out by Henry occurred about ten years later when he was invited to give a series of lectures on "God and the Modern Mind" at Willamette University in Salem, Oregon.

He was a member of the faculty at Fuller Seminary at the time. (Henry was acting dean there in 1947 and a professor between 1947 and 1956.) The invitation, as far as Henry could tell, came from the Willamette campus chapter of the Inter-Varsity Christian Fellowship. When he arrived in Salem, two students met him and drove him to a nearby hamburger stand for a bite to eat before moving on to the university, where Henry was scheduled to speak.

"We couldn't have been more thrilled to get your letter of acceptance saying you'd speak," they told him. "But we should confess that we two students are the whole Inter-Varsity effort here, and we've been worrying about how we can pay your travel expenses. We've lined up a junior-high-school auditorium that seats twelve hundred. But we didn't get out any newspaper publicity. Only two posters got put up."

To make matters worse, Henry's lectures were scheduled simultaneously and competitively with the events of Religious Emphasis Week on campus. The students, again with good intentions, had hoped to inject an evangelical flavor into the proceedings by inviting Henry.

Henry swung into action quickly when the boys told him the unvarnished facts. He switched the meeting place from the auditorium to a small room that could hold only 150 people. "The auditorium would have been an unpopulated desert," Henry laughs now.

When 175 persons showed up, creating a standing-room-only crowd, the event was proclaimed a success.

In fact, the lectures were so well received that at the end of the week, the university president asked Henry if he would join the philosophy department the following year. Henry declined.

Another bonus: Now-Senator Mark Hatfield of Oregon attended Henry's lectures and later said that Henry was an instrumental force in his own Christian growth.

GOD WORKED

"God worked in that situation and once again vindicated the truth of Romans 8:28," Henry believes. "There were potential problems: The lectures might have been a reproach on the Lord's work because the means to make them successful were neglected. And there was the rivalry with the official university program of Religious Emphasis Week.

"But the inexpertise of the two students, one of them Doug Coe, now a leader of Fellowship House in Washington D.C. and instrumental in arranging the annual Presidential Prayer Breakfasts, was overruled by the sincere faith they had in God."

Henry believes the incident illustrates how God can be trusted in a situation with many embarrassing overtones. God used it as a means to good.

Carl, the two students, and a small remnant of Christians on campus joined together in prayer to turn the situation around.

"Through intercessory prayer," Henry recollects, "we claimed God's promise to honor a witness to the truth. And we were emboldened by the legitimate place to which the whole truth is entitled in an academic environment."

It was to be a lesson which emboldened Carl F. H. Henry many times in future years when he stood before secular throngs in classrooms, lecture halls, and television appearances.

Perhaps the most acute crisis faced by Henry was a vocational one. It surrounded his coming to and going from *Christianity Today* magazine.

Admitting that he had no reluctance accepting the invitation to go to Washington, D.C., in 1956 to become founding editor of the journal, Henry says his theological and journalistic backgrounds made such a choice natural.

The crunch came when the board asked him to stay permanently. The rub was whether to return to Fuller, which was ideal for pursuing book-writing and the academic realm, or to settle for the more journalistically oriented *Christianity Today* editorship.

Though, by its third year, *Christianity Today* was off to a good start and had already eclipsed the liberal *Christian Century* in circulation, Henry saw the editorship slot as "an endless job always without adequate editorial personnel."

"It was like going through a funeral," Carl lamented as he relived the decision as we talked in the late afternoon sunlight on the sun deck of his suburban Washington home. "I felt like Carl Henry in some sense died after my second year at *Christianity Today* and a commitment was made to stay. I had once thought that to go back into journalism was a possible betrayal of my calling; but now I took a decisive turn from academic priorities."

But the bottom line was knowing it was God's will to take the job for what, as far as Henry knew, might be the rest of his career.

Having written a letter accepting the post, Henry drove the mile to the post office, one hand on the steering wheel, the other tightly holding the hand of his wife, Helga, who sat close beside him. They said nothing. The letter fluttered into the mail slot. The course of the Henrys' lives was changed—and undoubtedly so was the course of evangelical Christianity in this country, if not the world.

CHRISTIANITY TODAY

Ten years later, *Christianity Today* was firmly established as a flagship magazine of thinking people's evangelical Christianity. Henry had a paid circulation of

160,000 for the biweekly. But he also faced what seemed to be nearly unbearably heavy responsibilities for the editorial staff.

About a year later Henry was "dreaming of academic alternatives," to use the erudite but usual lucid language he chooses to describe things.

But what shocked him in 1967 was receiving letters from Christian leaders in three overseas countries saying they were sorry to hear that Henry was leaving *Christianity Today* and that the board was searching for a replacement.

This, of course, was a total surprise to Henry. So he wrote back, assuring them there was nothing to it.

But what happened in August 1967 came as such a shock to Henry, who stands six-foot-two and weighed 218 pounds at the time, that he lost over thirty pounds in the following months. Through a routine physical checkup at the Mayo Clinic in Rochester, Minnesota, medics asked about the sharp loss of weight.

"I was disappointed by some Christian friends," I told the doctor, "and lost faith in them. That is all I want to say about it."

The *it* Henry was reluctant then—and now—to speak about was the way the executive committee, in private meetings, decided to replace Henry with a new editor. A letter from the chairman told Henry he would be released from the job after one more year.

"It was written as if I were seeking to be free," Henry said, adding that, "the other board members, when informed of the matter, were as shocked as I was."

In fact, as Henry tells it, when the full board met at the end of the year, a majority agreed—and in the presence of the executive committee—that if Carl would consent, it would be happy to have him continue as editor for life.

Though Henry prefers not to speak publicly about the executive committee's reasons for wanting him ousted, it is known in evangelical inner circles that some felt that he was too soft on ecumenical church groups and not agressive enough in support of the conservative right.

To Henry, however, the damage had been done. Not only was he hesitant to make a life-time commitment to the editorship, a condition not part of his previous commitment to *Christianity Today*, he also felt he could never again recover a healthy relationship with the executive committee.

The day he got the letter from the board chairman, who also was chairman of the executive committee, Henry recalled a heartfelt talk he had had with Helga one night as the two walked, hand in hand, through the moonlit streets of Wheaton. They were in love, talking about life together. "There may well be two or three dark times in my life, Helga, and I'll have to lean heavily on you then," Carl had said.

When he told Helga the news at the dinner table that summer night in 1967, Carl prefaced it by saying there would be two ways to look at it:

One, they had previously talked about a return sometime to a campus and teaching career. "Now, God has providentially opened that door to the kind of vocation we have always loved. It has come about two or three years earlier than we had thought."

The other way of looking at the news was terse. Henry explained: "I have lost my job as editor of *Christianity Today*."

Neither Carl nor Helga wept. But they were perplexed.

"Helga has a strong trust in God's power and has helped me to multiply my ministry," Carl said later. "Through her own literary and academic gifts and her insights she provides rich shared topics of conversation."

Mrs. Henry, a faithful letter writer, has world mission interests and is a godly woman of prayer and faith.

After prayer, Henry decided to turn down inquiries about joining faculties at both religious and secular colleges. Instead, Carl and Helga took a year out to go to Cambridge University in England to pursue scholarly study and writing.

Though Henry was clearly told he was to have no future voice in the editorial policy of *Christianity Today*, he was asked to be an editor-at-large and to write a periodic column called "Footnotes." He continued this until it was terminated just before the departure of his successor, Harold Lindsell, *Christianity Today's* editor from 1968 to early 1978.

Looking back at the vocational crisis a decade later, Henry summed up: "We were more disenchanted and disillusioned than we were crushed. I knew God had a purpose—He could vindicate. For the moment it seemed difficult to see how this could be a door to an equally useful ministry."

Carl shared the news about *Christianity Today* first with his children Paul and Carol, very openly and with confidence. "We knew they stood with us in prayer. The spiritual shock that I endured was nothing in the way of a psychic disturbance. I never became bitter. It never in any way weakened my faith in God. The disappointment was wholly with men in certain evangelical associations."

And paraphrasing a thought from Reinhold Niebuhr's *Moral Man and Immoral Society*, Henry added: "Men acting in groups sometimes engage in actions they would not pursue in personal dealings with their neighbor."

Turning to how the dark strands of life's tapestry can be woven into a brighter pattern of God's handiwork, Henry recounted how he has walked the streets with other men who have lost their jobs as college presidents and other professional positions, counseling them.

LEAN HEAVILY ON BIBLICAL ASSURANCE

Said Henry: "I have urged them to lean heavily on the biblical assurance that nothing touches the life of one of God's committed servants. Out of it God will bring what glorifies Him and is good for His servant, and through his servant what best serves his fellow man.

"That conviction gives a balance, a perspective, and even an inexplicable secret joy in the midst of disappointment and disenchantment.

"Looking back today, I would have to say that the outlines for the second and third and even the fourth volumes of *God, Revelation & Authority* took shape at Cambridge. I sank myself deeply into theological literature in a way I could not have done along with the magazine responsibility. The beginnings of the four-volume tome got under way then, and that has been my central interest since."

Henry returned from Britain to serve a stint as a professor at Eastern Baptist Theological Seminary in Philadelphia and, more recently, as lecturer-at-large for World Vision International, the humanitarian Christian relief organization headquartered in Monrovia, California.

But, cautioned Henry, when I asked him if he might have had even greater effectiveness had he stayed in mass media from the start, "One cannot decide what he ought to do from the standpoint of latter years but only in good conscience and in seeking the will of God along the way. And that I tried to do."

The question for a Christian, summed up Henry as we sensed from the delicious aroma wafting from Helga's kitchen that dinner would soon be served, is not how to have the greatest influence or leadership but how to obey God.

"I never aspired to leadership," Henry averred. "Leadership is God's gift and God provides it. And when He does it is in the arenas that He gives, and He determines the seasons for which it is given.

"What God asks is obedience, not prominence or even success."

Where does the theologian-author, who knows and understands the Bible at a depth matched by few, turn for spiritual help and sustenance? "It's a triple track," Henry replied:

"(1) personal and family devotions; (2) a Friday night prayer cell, made up of young and professional people, who meet in different neighborhood homes, frequently ours; (3) Bible investigative work carried out for my own research and writing."

Elaborating on the need for personal prayer, Henry spoke not with the intellectualism of a theological giant but with the simple faith of a humble believer:

"A good season of prayer on one's knees in which one pours out his heart to God is always to me a thoroughly cleansing and refreshing experience. One sees the whole of life in relationship to the rule of God in his life and the Lordship of Christ. In a time of sustained personal prayer there is the deepest and most profound tie to the ultimately real world."

It is in these times of praying alone—"Gethsemane prayer," Carl calls it—when one isn't ashamed to shed tears, that he has felt the guidance of the Lord in life's toughest decisions.

ANXIETIES, NOT DOUBTS

Doubts? These, Carl says, he's never had, at least regarding his own assurance of salvation and commitment to Christ. But anxieties? "These I've always had," he added, hastening to explain that he is, in a sense, talking about *professional anxiety.*

There is, he says as a theologian, a kind of intellectual doubt one assumes in theological probing to examine the strengths and weaknesses of alternative commitments.

"It is the desire, therefore, to bear witness to the truth with integrity, in love, and to avoid a polemical harshness that repels," he elucidated. "Yet, I find God turns those anxieties, if one resolves them in prayer and trust, into a winsome personal dynamic."

Professional anxiety, for Henry, is akin to the way he experiences doubt. He frequently speaks to groups whose philosophical suppositions are very alien to evangelicalism. Then, his concern is that what he says will be formed in such a way that the truth and relevance of the Christian perspective is set forth clearly and convincingly.

"I am concerned for truth and fidelity in presenting my message to a particular audience. Since the comprehension level of the audiences I speak to varies greatly, part of my anxiety is that I not miss the level of that audience."

Emotionally, Henry glides along pretty much on an even keel. If anything tends to upset him, it's when he feels overcommitted and staggered by deadlines and multiple tasks. His mail is heavy, uncontrolled, and unpredictable. When he is swamped by an overload, he tends to feel paralyzed intellectually and tightened up so that he doesn't do his best work.

And, the tendency to overcommit may have been a factor in the stabbing migraine headaches Carl suffered for years.

Dispensing a prescription which has helped him and at long last has eliminated the migraines and which is applicable to all, Henry declared:

"The problem is not long range. Every day is a gift of God. Life is a gift. Life in Christ is a gift, and God doesn't expect us to do more than one thing at a time.

"So set your priorities. Arrange them in terms of what needs to be done. God always gives us enough time to do the things He really wants us to do. Some commitments could be done as well or better by others with an evangelical commitment. We are not all that indispensable to each and every project in the church of Christ."

As Carl Henry sees it, the places of privilege in Christ's

kingdom are not reserved for those who aspire to sit on top of the world.

So it is not a question of sitting on top of the world all the time, even if one could. Or at *any* time. Rather, Christ belongs at the top of the world. He is the king of the cosmos.

"It is well to remember our finitude and our sinfulness," advises Henry, "even in the midst of our present regeneration. All we have and are and can hope to be issues from the sovereignty and the righteousness and holiness and grace of our Redeemer.

"The Christian is promised no exemption from pain, sorrow, or disappointment. We are not called upon by the Gospel to live with a cultivated smile."

Eschewing all phony piety, Henry exhorts the true follower of Christ to show confidence in God and to trust in the midst of vicissitudes.

"I've known the sorrow of bereavement, the driving, unrelenting pain of migraines. I've known the uncertainties of surgery," Henry said as he concluded the final interview in his living room the next morning.

"And I know the time will soon come when I must lay down my pen and go to that world where the Word of God no longer needs human witnesses.

"In all these experiences, the dynamic presence and power of the Risen Lord is fully adequate."

To Carl F. H. Henry, and to hosts of those who would also follow the Christ he serves, these are the marks of an authentic faith.

*Bill and
Gloria Gaither*

3

They Just Praise the Lord

Bill and Gloria Gaither are both poets and lovers of the world. Through the artistry of their Christian music they are reaching the world with the message of God's love.

The Bill Gaither Trio, which includes Bill, Gloria, and Gary McSpadden, has become one of America's most sought-after Christian singing groups. Bill and Gloria are among the best known husband and wife songwriting teams today. Their more than 250 songs include "He Touched Me," "Let's Just Praise the Lord," "Because He Lives," "The Family of God," and "There's Something About That Name."

These, plus "The King Is Coming," "Something Good Is About to Happen," and dozens of gospel songs written for children, like "God Loves to Talk to Little Boys While They're Fishin'," have been turned out at the Gaithers' living-room Baldwin in their hometown of Alexandria, Indiana, a midwestern farm community of 6,000.

Success certainly has come to songwriter, bass, and

pianist Bill, and blonde, lyricist-alto Gloria. But you wouldn't know it from talking to them. They are not apt to tell you that the Gaither Trio has dominated the Gospel Music Association's annual Dove Awards for the past few years, or that Bill was Songwriter of the Year for five years running. If you pressed them, they might mention that they won Grammy awards in 1974 and 1975 and that "Because He Lives" was the 1976 Gospel Song of the Year.

JUST PLAIN FOLKS

Bill and Gloria Gaither are just plain folks. Christians who are part of the family of God, they say. And they would rather talk about living the Christian faith in practical ways—loving each other and their three children and trying to be more like Jesus—than anything else.

"The number of copies of sheet music and records are not the big thing to us," Bill told a reporter for the *Saturday Evening Post,* which did a four-page spread on the Gaithers in April 1977. "It's the knowing that there are people out there who've been through the things we've been through, the things that have changed our lives, and that somehow we're able to communicate with them—to share."

Christian faith has been central to Bill and Gloria ever since they were tiny. Bill, born in March 1936 in Alexandria, and Gloria, born six years later in Battle Creek, Michigan, were both raised as church kids, they told me as we visited at the Indianapolis airport, an hour's drive from Alexandria.

Their conversions, as such, were not big and dramatic, though Gloria vividly remembers making a commitment to Christ when she was not quite five years old.

"A child really can understand and be saved at a young age," she said earnestly, crinkling at the corners of her blue eyes. "I heard the Bible read aloud every night in my Christian home. But one night, when it was time for me to pray aloud at my turn, I couldn't do it. I knew I wasn't a Christian in my heart."

Once that had been explained, she was able to invite Jesus into her heart. Her conscience has "stayed very sensitive ever since. I went to the altar many times."

Gloria was reared in the Church of God and Bill in the Church of the Nazarene. They both attended Anderson College in Anderson, Indiana, and became teachers. But they didn't meet until Bill had been out teaching high-school English for four years. Gloria occasionally substituted at Bill's school.

TIME OF INTELLECTUAL QUESTIONING

For both Gloria and Bill, college was a time of intellectual questioning, a time of reexamining the Christian commitment they had made as children.

Bill described the mental rebellion of his early twenties, though it was nothing really overt. The result was a "definite commitment in a crisis experience," however. "It was time to get serious about this whole matter of being a Christian, and doubts are a hard thing for an evangelical kid to explain to others," Bill volunteered.

From that time onward, Bill's decisions have been based on his commitment to Christ.

Gloria described going through a labyrinth of doubt and upheaval in college. The heart of it was wondering whether she had accepted Christ as part of her cultural context rather than because of the reality of His salvation and power.

"What tipped the boat for me were the 'old saints' I had known as I was growing up," Gloria said. She compared the final outcome of their faith to the final outcome for people who embraced cynicism.

"It was not so much the flashy people," she continued, "the preachers or evangelists, as much as the old people who had served the Lord for years and years and years

and years. I had seen the final outcome of that commitment and what it had made of them and I also saw what
nonbelieving finally did. It was the closest thing to a test
tube to see the lives and the final results."

Gloria's biggest crisis didn't happen until she was well
into adult life. The struggle, she said, was "just being a
Christian. I used all my energy just keeping on an even
keel. I was a nervous Christian. I reviewed my life
nightly."

Then it dawned on Gloria that though she had accepted
Jesus as her Saviour, she had never really made Him Lord
of her life.

THE LORDSHIP OF CHRIST

"Resolving the Lordship of Christ was a giant thing,"
she stressed. Doing so gave her an anchor. It took away
"so many nebulous, gray areas that took so much strength
and energy." She was able to lie back in the love of God
and channel some of her energies into helping and nurtur-
ing others.

"I realized I was not just a consumer, but a vessel," she
said succinctly.

"Letting go and letting God wasn't easy," Gloria remembers, "because it meant releasing Bill and the children and things I had been dealing with in my own
power."

Looking back, she observed: "When you let go of everything and invest everything—sink or swim, live or
die—in the Lordship of Christ, then I really believe the
only kind of growth that happens comes as a result of
obedience.

"He who believes, obeys; and he who obeys, believes,"
she said, referring to a basic tenet of the German theologian Dietrich Bonhoeffer. "It doesn't matter if your whole
world falls in, financially or socially or even profession-
ally, for you can look God in the face and say, 'I did what

You said,' and there's a joy. You take the gut-level risk, and then comes the joy, happiness and assurance."

Bill and Gloria seem absolutely convinced the Lordship question is the primary one for every Christian. Until that is settled, they feel, a believer is bound to be bothered by indecision and the tug of wanting to follow Jesus while at the same time desiring approval from the world.

"The risk of being misunderstood by people is not fun," interjected Bill. "We all want to be loved."

"Yes," said Gloria, "but you don't say to God, 'You show me so I won't make a fool of myself, and then I'll believe.' The leap of faith comes first, and then comes knowledge."

As was true for many of their hymns and gospel songs, the words to "I Believe; Help Thou My Unbelief" came out of the daily experience of living their faith:

> I long so much to feel the warmth
> That others seem to know;
> But should I never feel a thing,
> I claim Him even so!
> > *I Believe, Help Thou My Unbelief,*
> > © Copyright 1975 William J. Gaither

"Hundreds of times we have felt that melting presence, in an almost tangible touch of a wave," said Gloria with a natural touch of poetry. "But when the tide flows out, we have to know it's there just the same."

Bill and Gloria believe that once they settled the Lordship question they have been able to deal with everyday issues "more rationally, more fairly, and more head-on" because of the inner security they feel.

According to Gloria, her doubts and questions now center on procedural points, like, "How should I work with You, God? How long should I wait? How, Lord, are You going to do this?"

DOUBTS NO LONGER OF GOD

"My doubts," Bill added, "are at the point of saying, 'Did I do that for the right reason?' Our doubts are no longer on God, but on ourselves. Now, it's choosing between better, best, and 'best of best.' "

The Gaithers see the stewardship of time as a major problem with which they must constantly battle. When Christian values do not coincide with those of the world, how do they judge the most important things in life?

For example, the day I interviewed Bill and Gloria at the Indianapolis airport they had just returned from a short—and unusual for them—vacation trip without their kids.

The big decision on that morning, the first time they were back together as a family, had been to plan family time together. They decided to spend the morning going out to their pasture with their children, aged twelve, eight, and seven, bridling up the horses and riding, and then going over to Bill's parents' home for the noon meal.

"We have to schedule time to make things like that happen," noted Gloria.

"How do you know you are making the right decisions?" I asked this friendly couple whose personalities seem to complement each other so well.

"Decision-making takes a lot of energy," replied Bill. "Also time. And some decisions need to be made—and finished. It's senseless going over the same ground once a basic decision has been made."

FINDING GOD'S GUIDANCE

He went on to relate how he and Gloria had just made a major decision that involved their professional careers. They followed a series of steps which he said they had found practical at other times to determine God's guidance:

First, consult three or four spiritual people, counselors whose opinion you trust: "Surround yourself with persons who will be honest."

Second, consult the Scriptures: "There's so much wisdom there."

In particular, Gloria and Bill said, there is wisdom in the Book of Proverbs, the Prophet Isaiah, in studying the way Jesus dealt with problems, and in Paul's instructions to Timothy.

Third, said Bill, *pray!*

Fourth, ask yourself some hard questions, such as "Do I measure up?" "Am I doing this for the right reason?" Check your motives.

Fifth, "sleep on it." Reexamine the matter again four or five days later.

And finally, make the decision, "even if it involves risk and it might appear to be failure in the world's eyes."

Regarding a professional decision he and Gloria had made that he did not want to share, Bill said they had thought it through very carefully, making sure the reasoning process they had used to arrive at the decision had been right in God's sight.

"The decision *was* right," Bill concluded. "We have peace in our souls."

"To make spiritual decisions where not everyone is happy is difficult," Gloria broke in. "Discipleship may not be the popular thing, but the Word of God has to be our bottom line. It is the absolute authority against which we measure everything, not what is going on in the world.

"We live in a world, a culture, that has no bottom line. The social bottom line is now gone. If you don't have some kind of a lifeguard stand to measure against, you don't even know you've drifted."

It was Bill's turn to break into the conversation. He backed up Gloria's point by quoting from one of their songs—"a fun song, with a barb"—which speaks about the absurdity of "arranging the pictures on the wall when the house is burning down."

Our values can become twisted to the wrong standards at home, too, the Gaithers assert. Always reassessing their priorities, they put serving the Lord as good parents at the top of their list, followed by writing music, recording, and performing, in that order. That ranking means the Gaither Trio turns down nine out of every ten invitations to sing, and they rarely travel out of town during the week.

It also means that the decision-making process the Gaithers use for professional-type decisions also applies to ones at home.

BASIC DECISIONS APPLIED DAILY

Basic decisions were made long ago, though they must be applied daily, Gloria explained. Thus the Gaithers' emphasis on developing strong Christian character in Suzanna, Amy, and Benjj is applied when it comes to settling an argument, or planning for piano lessons or a Little League ball game.

"Our aims for the kids are that they become mature Christian people in a real world," said Bill. "And make decisions even though they're costly," said Gloria, adding that she recognizes that it is not possible to expect immature people (children) to make mature (adult) decisions.

The Gaithers' interest in improving the self-image of their own children has worked its way into some of their songs and into Gloria's two books based on experiences of home and children, *Rainbows Live at Easter* and *Make Warm Noises*.

One of the Gaithers' children's songs says:

> I am a promise, I am a possibility.
> I am a promise, with a capital P.
> I'm a great big bundle of potentiality.

I Am a Promise, © Copyright 1975 William J. Gaither

Bill and Gloria trust God to take care of their children. And that if their home life is meaningful, the children's future will be, too.

"Just because we're Christians, we're not infallible," commented Gloria, as we turned to the topic of overcoming anxiety and where Christians can find spiritual resources in time of need.

"We need to go back and say, 'We were wrong.' We need to be sensitive to God's will. For the oil of the Holy Spirit to flow back into our lives we have to do that," Gloria asserted.

ANXIETIES FOLLOW DISOBEDIENCE

Anxieties follow disobedience to God, Bill believes. "We don't always trust the processes of God. We get impatient and anxious. We sometimes say, in a joking sort of way, 'I sure hope God knows what He's doing!' "

Bill went on to talk about doubts in the framework of his "beating on some doors, finally breaking them down, just to see if God really knew what He was doing."

When Bill had forced God's hand, however, he realized that he should have been willing for God, in His time, to open the doors that He had closed.

In that case, Bill declared, he approached God in confession and asked forgiveness, saying, "I'm sorry, I was out of Your will."

Waiting is the hardest thing for Gloria. "It's that internal struggle that just kills you because it saps so much of your energy. Once God shows you what to do, the doing is never that hard."

She also finds herself "taking things back after committing them to the Lord"—a failing with which many of us can readily identify. "I shouldn't worry, but I do!" confessed Gloria.

"I think the devil is the accuser in getting you generally frustrated," chimed in Bill. "When you feel that great, gray, nebulous ball of something wrong, it's generally Satan. But when God accuses, it's specific—who, what, where. But wallowing in a problem doesn't help anything."

Gloria added an insight she and Bill gained from reading old diaries that described events in the Gaithers' lives six or seven years earlier. In retrospect, she observed, things that appeared to be major crises at the time the diaries were written turned out to be less important later. But the happy "little incidents"—as seen then—turned out to be "the big, giant things we almost missed, they were so regular, so daily."

What seem so often to be big, dark, rain clouds now, turn out to pass overhead with only a few drops of moisture. "But if we are absorbed by the threat of the storm, we may miss seeing the rainbow.

"At the ripe old age of forty-one," concluded Bill, "I know there are some things in life I cannot change. All I can change is my attitude to them."

Then, pausing, he added that he did not mean that he should not do his best to effect change. And, he admitted, it's always hard to know when he is waiting on the Lord, and when he's copping out: "Have you knocked long enough, or do you now have the crowbar out to break in the door? What *is* knocking long enough? What is trying hard enough? What is walking away too soon?"

The couple concluded that the only way to know the

answers to questions like these is to "test the spirits"—
after looking at whatever objective data is available.

READ THE WORD

"You have to read the Word over and over and over,"
declared Gloria. "That's the number one thing."

She singled out the Old Testament Book of Isaiah. "It's
been pure honey to me this summer," she said, "and the
Gospels, which feed the reader with what Jesus said,
what He was about, what He told us to do, how He felt,
how He reacted. Really get to know the overall Person of
Christ, and then stack that up against the situation you
face."

Both Bill and Gloria cautioned against putting too much
emphasis on feelings, though they are important to cor-
roborate or deny objective scriptural data from a spiritual
standpoint.

"When there's hocus-pocus chemistry in the air, God
gets blamed for a lot of things He didn't do—like the
person who eats twenty-five green apples and then has
someone pray for his belly ache," added Gloria with a
laugh.

Next to the Scriptures, the Gaithers rank going to the
family of God—mature, wise, stable believers—as the
most important spiritual resource available to Christians.

"We need to be nurtured along in the family. The family of God has to be directive," explained Gloria. "The
family of believers is where you go for help."

Although the third source of spiritual help Bill and
Gloria mentioned would be natural for two songwriters, it
is equally available to all Christians—hymns by lyricists
of the past like Fanny Crosby and Philip P. Bliss.

And, it might be added, the Gaithers' songs have been
an inspiration and source of strength and comfort to millions of contemporary Christians.

Bill and Gloria, aware of this, nonetheless are awed by
it.

"We knew our songs were special and God-given," said Bill. "We knew that in our souls when we were struggling songwriters. But the important thing was that we had emptied our souls of something special."

Once the Gaither Trio grew successful, there was the added "excitement of being used."

Realizing that a crowd of 10,000 people at a Gaither concert are singing their songs because the melodies and words have become a part of their lives can be most rewarding.

Bill told of a young father who came up to the Gaithers after a concert in Toronto to thank them for the contemporary song of praise "Because He Lives."

"We just buried our six-year-old son," the man said. "He was run over while he was riding his bicycle. If it hadn't been for that song, I wouldn't have made it."

"When the honest sounds of Gaither music become a resource to pull others out of crisis, well," says Gloria, "that's the greatest pleasure, the biggest thrill of all."

Edward Victor Hill

4

Hang in There, Brother

I drove to the edge of Watts, the black sector of Los Angeles that erupted during the civil rights disturbances of the 1960s. Arriving at Mount Zion Missionary Baptist Church, I was soon escorted into the downstairs office of the pastor, the Reverend Edward Victor Hill.

Hill was on the phone coordinating a parade his church was sponsoring that Saturday. There were going to be at least 150 entries.

"Your participation and presence is a must. No one can fail," commanded the hulking, affable Negro pastor who is known the world over for his persuasive preaching and his conservative politics.

As I waited, I studied Hill's study. Books, papers, boxes, and magazines were piled and strewn everywhere. Only the chair I was sitting on and the one occupied by

Hill's imposing frame were clear of clutter.

"This is being done as a standup for Jesus," Hill was saying on the phone to someone who apparently needed a little coaxing to become a wholehearted supporter of the parade. "So let's stand up for Jesus!"

HANG IN THERE, BABY

Now my eyes fell on a poster on the corner wall. It was a cat, chinning himself on a bar. Underneath, it said: "Hang in there, Baby!"

That, I thought, was a good summary of E. V. Hill's struggle in life: the personal pilgrimage of a black man in twentieth-century America; a boy born and reared in southern Texas in poverty; a young student, assisted by a scholarship, gaining an education in a world where separate, though not quite equal, opportunities existed; a man, called to preach the Gospel, reconciling the two worlds, black and white, into one world which must become the Kingdom of his Lord and Savior, Jesus Christ. And because of Him, Hill has hung in there.

Hill hung up the phone and smiled. He knew I had been scrutinizing his office.

"My staff is embarrassed about this place," he said. "But I know what I'm doing. I just say, 'Come on in if you can *get* in!' "

Hill's easygoing manner immediately set me at ease. We chatted for a few moments about the fact that he often wears overalls to the church and likes to farm on his small place in the country.

"I like jokes and I love people," added Hill. That was already obvious.

And despite the apparent nearly total disarray and disorganization of his office, I found E. V. Hill to be one of the most organized persons I interviewed for this book.

When I asked him about the crises of his life, he me-

thodically and chronologically checked off twelve peaks
and valleys:

HIS PEAKS AND VALLEYS

(1) childhood; (2) entrance into college; (3) call to the
ministry; (4) becoming president of the National Baptist
Youth Convention; (5) his first full-time church; (6)
involvement in civil rights and politics, (7) leaving Houston for California; (8) becoming pastor of Mount Zion
Baptist Church, Los Angeles; (9) conflict with the Los
Angeles community—a great struggle, (10) "antiblac-
kism," which he later defined; (11) being a conservative
Republican—and Negro; and, (12) relationships with the
white community.

Conflict over race has been a major thread running
through much of Hill's career. But he is upbeat, not bitter,
about it.

"I am still an advocator of developing a strong racial
group of people," Hill has written in the *Baptist Student*
magazine (January, 1968). "But this is no longer done to
beat someone or to rule over someone. This is because I
now want to lead the Negro people to the many opportunities and the great fellowship of the third world—the
Christian world. I am still an avowed opponent of discrimination and segregation and despise those who try to
justify its continuance, even with the Bible. But I now
look upon them with pity, sympathy, and anxiousness to
impart to them or to see that they receive the knowledge
of the Lord Jesus Christ."

Except for the grace of God, Hill might have turned out
to be an angry black militant.

EARLY YEARS

Born in 1933 in Columbus, Texas, to parents who separated when he was one year old, Hill was reared by his

mother until he was age four. She made do on twelve dollars a week without welfare payments. By the time he was eleven, Edward moved to the country with the Langram family, where he lived in a two-room log cabin but enjoyed fresh milk and peanuts. Before he had graduated from the local four-teacher school in the Negro community of Sweet Home, Hill had learned how to earn his keep through hard work for Momma Langram and others. He stoked stoves, milked cows, picked cotton, harvested peanuts, processed molasses, and killed hogs.

"How did we make it?" Hill asked rhetorically. "I look back with fear and yet a great deal of rejoicing. The people feared God and we made it."

During his childhood, Hill was very active in church activities. He says he was "born again" when he was eleven. At the same time, however, he admits having "great problems with segregation . . . I doubted that white people were saved."

Because he was barred from showing his champion hogs in livestock fairs and shows against hogs entered by whites, Hill began to desire more than the black world could offer him. He rebelled at the idea that there had to be separate black and white worlds, on the excuse that blacks were on a lower level because of disease and lack of education.

"It would not have been hard for me to have become a follower of Black Muslim Elijah Mohammed," Hill confided during our interview, "or to call white people 'blue-eyed devils.' Who but lost people would have perpetrated what was put on us Negro people?"

A resolution of that crisis and the introduction of several new ones happened in 1951 when Hill, with a total of five dollars, arrived as a freshman at Prairie View College, the Negro part of the Texas A & M University system at that time.

When he learned he needed eighty dollars to enroll,

"faith was still strong, but doubt was speaking," Hill confessed. Fortunately, he soon discovered a Jesse Jones
scholarship for exceptional achievement as a high-school
student would pay all his expenses for four years.

The first semester, however, ended with two great
calamities: he lost the scholarship and his high-school
sweetheart. There was good news, too, though. Hill said
yes to God's call to become a preacher.

Twice before he had felt called of the Lord to preach;
once at the time of his conversion, and again the Sunday
night he received his high-school diploma. Each time,
Hill had used the excuse of his need for education to put
off the Lord.

If God would see to it that he was accepted into college,
then he would agree to be a preacher, Hill had said. But
now that he had a four-year scholarship, Hill felt he could
inform the Almighty he wouldn't be a minister after all.

"GOD DROPPED ME"

"God dropped me like a hot potato!" Hill chuckled
heartily. "In six weeks the bottom dropped out on me."

During that time, as a beginning freshman, Edward
confessed he drank, stole, and saw his grades go down
the tubes.

"I cried out to God and He heard me and picked me up
and I did start preaching," Hill continued. "Negro
preachers took me on as their project and as their son and
I drew large crowds as a boy preacher."

He went on to preach at revivals and in country and
storefront churches. For four years Hill was national
president of the National Baptist Youth Convention.

Because of his involvement with the Baptist Student
Union, Edward met a man used by God to change Hill's
whole attitude towards association with white Christians.

Hill and another Negro youth were selected to go with
three white students from Texas A & M to a national BSU

convention. The man responsible for driving the students there was Dr. W. F. Howard, then director of student work for the Baptist General Convention of Texas.

"For the first time in my life I became acquainted with a white man who was Christian enough to take a stand and to stand with a black man who was a Christian," Hill recalled nearly twenty-five years later.

"While on the trip and at the meeting, I discovered that within this Christian world were some blacks and some whites who had been regenerated to a point that the color of a man's skin really made no difference. I also discovered there were whites who were constantly in their local churches working to rid themselves and their communities of prejudice and discrimination. There was no beating of drums; they were not seen in the headlines, but they were sincere."

With Hill's change of heart and his decision to preach, his heart felt a blow of a different kind: his high-school girl friend dumped him.

"I know what it means to have a broken heart," Hill said with a touch of nostalgia. Not until after he had completed college did God fully bind up that wound. Hill married Jane Coruthers, a graduate nurse at Texas Southern University. They have two children, Norva Rose, who attended Westmont college in Santa Barbara, and Edward V. Hill, Jr., a student in a Christian elementary school in Los Angeles.

FIRST PASTORATE

Although he was ordained a Baptist minister in late December of 1954, Hill's first full-time pastorate began in 1955 when he was called to Mount Corinth Missionary Baptist Church in Houston. Edward was twenty, single, and still in college—and still in debt.

A professional church of 216 members, Mount Corinth's power structure was totally against him, Hill remembers. The church officers considered him a mere inexperienced boy with no college degree. For the first six weeks of Hill's pastorate, many protested by giving very little money in the offering. But, smiled Hill, he was able to raise more funds in those six weeks than had ever before been raised in the history of the church.

Although his running battle with the church pillars continued for three years, "by far the bulk of the membership was with me," Hill recalls. And during the remaining three years he served Mount Corinth, Hill assembled the largest young people's group of any church in Texas.

During those years of the late 1950s, Hill became deeply involved in the nascent civil rights movement. He won the primary race for the Houston City Council. He was the first black man to do so. He was a board member of the National Association for the Advancement of Colored People and one of seven original board members of the Southern Christian Leadership Conference. In the latter capacity he nominated the late Dr. Martin Luther King for president of the SCLC.

Hill was active in the planning and executing of integration of Houston schools, buses, and lunch counters. This aroused antagonism, however, and Hill says constant threats were made on his life and house. Once, acid was thrown on his car. He required bodyguards for a six-month period.

Just as he was overcoming these trials and was achieving increasing recognition in his church and community, Hill suddenly felt the Lord was telling him to pull up stakes and move to Southern California.

A MAJOR CRISIS

This, in itself, was one of the twelve major crises in his life, Hill said. "It was difficult leaving the South. It was not an easy decision. I had won the battles. I wanted to stay and enjoy some of the fruits. Many of the young people in the church felt hurt about my going. They didn't understand. And I thought there would be nothing to do out in California. I thought Los Angeles was the land of the 'good times.' "

Little did Hill know he would have mountains of problems in LA. Soon there would be conflict with the community and difficulties to overcome at the church. Actually there was a repetition of the obstacles he had faced in Houston six years earlier.

Mount Zion Missionary Baptist Church had been embroiled in a court battle for five years. Creditors were in foreclosure proceedings when Hill arrived on the scene. Some $151,000 in lawsuits had been filed against the church. Though the sanctuary could seat 1,100 persons, there were only 585 members. An average Sunday attendance was 300. Mount Zion was—and is—located in a transient community on the edge of the Watts ghetto. The church has no wealthy members, according to Hill.

Basically, he believes, the conflict stems from his not being an *understood* person.

"I'm never given credit for 'meaning well,' " he explained. "My critics say I'm always stubborn, egotistical, overambitious, cutting other people's throats, impatient, pushing too fast."

This, coupled with what militant blacks in the community call Hill's *Uncle Tomism*, have made some struggles difficult.

"The younger ones don't feel at home with me; the older ones suspect me," sized up Hill. "That is both hurting and frustrating," he added. "Now I'm fighting to keep away from the arrogance of not caring."

Success can make a person lonely, Hill feels. If this is so, he has reason to feel that he has few close friends; however, his endeavors have flourished despite opposition.

His church has grown to 1,800 members with an operating budget of $300,000 and a total program budget of

$700,000. He is president of the California State Baptist Convention. He has preached at a host of major conventions and city-wide revivals, including the International Congress on World Evangelization in Lausanne, Switzerland, and the Baptist World Alliance in Stockholm. And he has preached at services in the White House East Room when Richard Nixon was president.

CONTINUING CONFLICTS

Yet, even with all these successes, Hill speaks of the continuing conflict of his own race doubting his sincerity as it relates to their own welfare.

Hill candidly admits he doesn't trust white liberals or believe in the sincerity of the Democratic party. He is convinced that Democratic social programs don't get people off welfare.

To make matters worse from the liberals' point of view, Hill makes no bones about supporting the police. And he fears there is a communist world takeover plot and plan.

"I actually believe in it," he said, wanting me to know he wasn't being facetious.

The crowning blow to the liberal and militant elements of his race is that Hill rebels against *blackism*.

Blackism, he explained, means "to make an almost idolatrous emphasis on color; to get one's rights by any means necessary, to replace the present establishment power with our black power, and in reality perpetuate the same system of injustices and vengeance."

"I'm not for blackism, I'm for all colors," Hill says. "We didn't have to *become* black. We were winning offices in politics, colleges, corporations, and so forth. As Negroes we were making more speed than we were able to adjust to. Then all of a sudden we turned black."

This, Hill feels, was counterproductive for the advancement of Negro people because it shifted the sympathy of the middle-of-the-road white man, who was agreeable to these advances, to the conservative side, be-

cause of the raw militancy and stridence of persons like
Stokely Carmichael and Angela Davis.

BRANDED *UNCLE TOM*

When Hill articulated this philosophy, he was immediately branded an *Uncle Tom* by many blacks. He says
he got more death threats in integrated LA than he did in
Ku Klux Texas.

It hurt Hill to be accused by his own people of selling
them out and not being concerned. Some young people
im the community abandoned him. And some members
of his church apologized to their friends about belonging
to Mount Zion.

But Hill kept hammering away, though he says he saw
some awful things happen.

The tide turned, he feels, about 1970 when he says he
had a vision. The Lord said to him, "Edward, you've
stood the test!"

Since then, Hill has devoted major emphasis on build-
ing a core team of 1,300 committed church members.
Thousands of persons have come down the aisle of Mount
Zion Church to confess Jesus Christ as their Saviour and
Lord—and to walk back into the world in service to Him.

E. V. Hill is known as a strict disciplinarian. For example, women cannot wear slacks or pants in his church. He
does not preach an easy Gospel with a quick way to
heaven.

Bill Seitz, a white student from Wheaton College, who
worked with Hill on the staff in the summer of 1977, put it
this way: "They know he's pro-America, propolice,
prolaw-and-order. And yet they keep coming—every age,
every profession, every color."

OVERCOMING BY SPIRITUAL STRENGTH

Where, I asked Hill, do you find the spiritual strength
for overcoming, for getting the victory, in all of this?

In typical fashion, pastor Hill reeled off a list of points, enumerating each one as he went along:

1. I believe God. Note there is no preposition *in*. There is a distinction.

2. I do not believe in having a religion which you turn to in a crisis. I've had the experience of seeing God already there with the answer *before* the crisis. There's never been a time in all my crises where I have not had, in that very hour, directions as to what God wanted. I've never had to call an *emergency session*.

To prepare spiritual resources for crises, Hill has studied the Bible intensely. He has sifted the Psalms, picking out verses of praise, prayer, and testimony. For many years Psalms 51 and 71 have been special reservoirs of trust for him.

"When you feel life has mistreated you, praise the Lord with Psalms," he said. "If you have the faith, God has the power."

Hill has also found help going through the Epistles and copying out all the instructions to believers, as well as in studying the composite Gospel narratives of Jesus' life.

3. I have always expected to suffer. I have expected it to be rough and tough. That has freed me from illusions of grandeur. I believe I'm the hardest critic E. V. Hill has, so most of the time I seldom blame anyone else.

4. I have not expected a whole lot. Yet God has blessed me exceedingly abundantly above anything I've dreamed. My attitude is, "I don't need to have that." I have been surprised and grateful when it has come. I haven't had personal big ambitions.

Hill's income in 1977 was about thirty thousand dollars, and he was buying a new house. He and Jane began

planning for that twenty years before, he said. Most of the
furniture in their living and dining rooms and in Hill's
office came out of junk yards and auctions, Hill laughed,
twirling his glasses. I knew he wasn't kidding—about the
church office, at least.

Hill added a word of practical advice on financial matters: "A man on one hundred dollars a week shouldn't try
for a Rolls Royce. My ups and downs financially and emotionally generally have centered on *miscalculations*. I go
from zero up to as far as the Lord takes me; many people
start with a hundred and then fall down."

5. I have tried to make sure what I have done is
related to the ministry to which I've been called.

E. V. Hill is persuaded that what has been sound guidance from the Lord for him will also work for others. In
closing our two-hour interview, he passed on three *rec-
ommendations:*

Believe God (not *in* God).
Prepare to suffer. He emphasized that people today
crumble at the least little thing: "Talk about carrying
a cross, it's carrying a feather that's killing them!"
Relax and live a simple life.

His closing recommendation seemed to be at odds with
what he said next:
"Keep on moving, don't ever stop, don't ever stop.
Maybe reduce speed, but plow right on, plow right on,
don't stop."
Perhaps this contrasts to "relax and live a simple life"
less than it first appears. Because E. V. Hill, like the cat on
his poster, has hung in there, tough but relishing every
minute.

Vonette Bright

5

Woman of Prayer

Christianity hasn't made a greater impact because people are not living what they profess, is the view of Vonette Bright, wife of William R. Bright, founder-president of Campus Crusade for Christ.

Certainly, Christians have problems, added the attractive speaker, author, mother of two sons, and Churchwoman of the Year for 1973. But if they will yield themselves to God, He will provide solutions. Those solutions, Vonette Zachary Bright has found, are in the Bible.

"His Word is positively packed with solutions," she said as we talked in the sunny den of the Bright's hillside home at the Arrowhead Springs world headquarters of Campus Crusade. "God's textbook to man is the Scriptures," continued Vonette. "As long as we follow those principles then we are going to find solutions."

To illustrate both her belief that the answers are in the Bible and that Christians can lead problem-solved lives if they practice what they profess, Vonette quoted 1 John 1:5–7 RSV: "This is the message we have heard from him and proclaim to you, that God is light and in him is no darkness at all. If we say we have fellowship with him while we walk in darkness, we lie and do not live according to the truth; but if we walk in the light, as he is in the light, we have fellowship with one another, and the blood of Jesus his Son cleanses us from all sin."

Vonette is the coordinator of the Great Commission Prayer Crusade, a strategy to unite Christians of America and the world in prayer. She also acts as official hostess for Campus Crusade, the noted evangelical organization whose headquarters are nestled in the foothills of the San Bernardino Mountains in Southern California. Much of her time is spent speaking to church, civic, and women's groups. She speaks and writes about personal experiences that proclaim the reality of Christ and the practical authority of God's Word for today's world.

The key to overcoming, Vonette is convinced, is in choosing to trust the Lord rather than to find a solution in one's own strength. The latter route, in her own case, leads her to anxiety and frustration, Vonette confided.

"My disposition gets out of kilter. I'm robbed of my security and radiance in my walk with Christ."

GOD, I *WILL* TRUST YOU

When that happens, she tries to "really cast myself at the feet of the Lord and pray, 'God, I *will* trust You in this.' As I have placed my faith securely in Him, God has given me the solution, always with a biblical basis."

It has taken Vonette many years to come to that point. In her biography, *For Such a Time as This* (Fleming H. Revell Company) she tells of her romance with Bill Bright growing out of a high-school friendship in Coweta, Oklahoma, where the two grew up. At first, when she learned of Bill's dedication to Christ and his desire to serve the Lord through a specialized ministry, she resisted. Then, on the eve of her engagement to Bill, Vonette was brought to the place of making her own commitment to Christ through a long discussion with the late Henrietta Mears, director of Christian education at the Hollywood Presbyterian Church.

"Much to Bill's delight and relief, and to my surprise, I made my commitment to Jesus Christ, a commitment which I thought I had made as a little girl but one which had long since lost its meaning and relevance in my life," she wrote in the chapter, "Not Enough to Last a Lifetime."

Though the early months of their marriage were happy and Bill and Vonette were able to enjoy much time together, Bill became increasingly busy. He combined seminary training at Fuller Seminary in Pasadena with his profitable fancy food and Epicurean business. In the fall of 1951, Bill sold another business in which he was engaged and the Brights launched Campus Crusade for Christ at the University of California, Los Angeles campus. Vonette resigned a teaching job to help him work with the young women.

Soon there were still more demands on Vonette's time. Their first son Zachary was born. After Bradley, the second son, was born, Vonette's household responsibilities increased again. By now, hundreds of students attending various crusade meetings were crowding into the Bel Air home the Brights were sharing with Miss Mears. "Keeping the house clean, organizing refreshments and being a good hostess were time consuming," Vonette remembers, "as was being an attentive, available wife and mother."

HOMEMAKER'S BLAHS

Like many a modern-day housewife, Vonette soon came down with all the symptoms of homemaker's blahs: dishes, diapers, and dust. She seemed chained to all the tedious, annoying tasks. She was bored, even a little resentful.

"After months of being filled with anxiety and frustration," Vonette wrote in her autobiography, "I began to wonder if I should seek professional counsel. As I harbored my discontent about the house and the work I had to do, my frustration and dissatisfaction mushroomed, engulfing other areas of my life. Soon my husband, my children, Miss Mears, and the students were as irritating to me as the house itself. I felt locked in a dull, monotonous, laborious existence without a key."

Still, Vonette told me as we sipped coffee on a warm August morning, she realized that decisions regarding marriage, children, and full- or part-time careers involve responsibility. And responsibility involves boring labor.

But all occupations have some boring routine, Vonette reasoned, so just escaping household chores wasn't the answer.

"The first thing I had to face was, where is the reality of the Christian life? And why am I resentful of doing the same jobs over and over again?"

Vonette came back to what she believes is the bedrock purpose of her life: to honor God and to bring glory to Him. She was then able to pray: "If I can honor You more, Lord, by doing dishes, laundering diapers, and cleaning this house, being totally in the background when I've been used to being in the foreground, then I will be willing—available—to do that."

Vonette flashed her ready smile. "I talked by the hour to myself and to the Lord telling Him that I was available to Him. I turned to the Scriptures where practical illustrations were given to me."

PRAYER, A *VITAL, VITAL* PART OF LIFE

Emphasizing that prayer has been a *vital, vital* part of her life, Vonette added, "I talk to God as my very best friend. I tell Him when I don't understand something and ask for His wisdom."

God did not take away the housework. He changed
Vonette's attitude. And that made all the difference, she
says. The irritations began to melt away. Little by little
Vonette came to understand the reality of the Christ-
controlled, spirit-filled life. She learned not to look at circumstances but at making herself available to God. Set-
ting her mind and affection on Christ, she gained the
victory.

There were other bridges to cross on her spirited journey toward spiritual maturity. "One," Vonette said candidly, "was to accept my husband's great dreams and
aspirations that seemed far too large for reality."

Anyone who knows Bill Bright and the scope of his
Campus Crusade ministry, the grueling travel pace he
sets for himself, and the long hours he devotes to fulfilling
the Great Commission in this decade, understands that
Vonette is married to a most unusual man.

"Here is a man who dared to trust God for great things
and God has dared to bring them about," Vonette said in
tribute to Bill. She says he has helped her more than anyone else in learning to trust God.

Ask Bill Bright if he has problems and he's likely to
reply, "What problems?" Because of his faith and his per-
sonality, Bill doesn't consider that he has problems.

"Bill can honestly say he has no problems," Vonette
feels, "because he so quickly hands problems over to
God. 'It's God's responsibility to work this out,' he says.
Then he relaxes or sleeps and goes on to cope with other
things."

Actually, in her opinion, "Bill Bright probably has more
problems than any man walking the face of the earth.
When you have six thousand staff members in one
hundred countries, you can't help but have problems."

By nature Bill is a carefree person, according to
psychological tests he has taken. He is not bothered by
anxieties. And he scored low in caring what other people

think. Vonette sees him as being more concerned about pleasing God than about pressure from people.

Vonette, on the other hand, scored in the middle ranges both in anxiety level and in caring what others think.

Knowing this difference between them has helped Vonette understand why Bill can submit to God more quickly and completely than she can. "I admit I get almost impatient with him when he tells me, 'You're not trusting God with this,' " Vonette added: "I know that he's right and that's what gets to me. But it also encourages me that he can trust God so fast. I'm learning from him."

Summing up, she declared: "Bill has this unique, natural disposition, plus a unique confidence in God's readiness to cope, which is available to every one of us."

"How does a person cultivate this?" I asked.

GOD LEADS US TO HELP

"God leads us to help through a person, a book, a Scripture verse, a sermon, an idea," Vonette responded. "But you have to be receptive, you have to be willing to do what He wants you to do."

Vonette believes the purpose of problems is to cause us to trust God more and to learn that He is adequate. Each problem that is conquered through trust in God enables us to have more faith so that we can trust Him with the next problem.

"Faith really grows by adversity brought into our lives," Vonette said. "God has a perfect solution, a perfect plan, a way out. Sometimes it is revealed quickly, and sometimes there is a waiting period."

Vonette needed two years in order to reach the point where she was willing to trust God in a stubborn situation involving fear.

She was afraid she was going to die.

The gnawing anxiety plagued her, and she was embarrassed to seek help for many months. Though she admitted the fear was mostly psychosomatic, in her mind, it nevertheless was very real. Vonette had not spoken publicly about her persistent fear of death. She described it to me as being like a Satanic attack—a spiritual affliction.

The fear began one day when Vonette was half asleep, thinking about a project revising a Campus Crusade staff training manual Bill had asked her to do. The task was difficult, and it would take a year's time to complete. As she contemplated the work, in a half-conscious state, she felt as if a little voice inside her were saying, "You'll never have opportunities to do these things again. You aren't going to be here. You only have two years to live."

At that time, Vonette was frequently alone, working on the writing project, as well as caring for her two small children. Psychologically, she said, she was ripe for such a problem to work its way into her mind.

"I decided to live radiantly, be happy, and then check out of life with a strong witness."

Several things reenforced Vonette's conception that something was seriously wrong with her and that she would soon die. One was a scar from a benign mole which she had had removed from her shoulder several years before. Though there was no apparent physical cause for it, Vonette kept feeling a funny sensation where the mole had been. "I was sure I had cancer," she recalled, amused now at the notion.

When Vonette heard Dr. Henry Brandt, a well-known Christian psychologist, speak on psychosomatic illnesses and say that Christians do suffer from them, she decided to talk personally to Brandt about her fear of the mole.

He told her how sin or inconsistencies in a Christian's life can produce illnesses which are without medical explanation. So Vonette tried to tell herself that the sensation in her shoulder wasn't there and that it was all in her imagination.

She saw her doctor, who said it must be psychosomatic.

"Beyond that, I was afraid to share the problem for fear I would be another example to be used by somebody— 'Pray for Vonette Bright; she's having spiritual problems!' "

Vonette now thinks her experience is rather common. She decided to share it in some detail with me in hopes that readers of this book would not feel they are strangely unique if they have similar fears about sickness or death.

HELP FROM THE BIBLE

Vonette did seek help from the Bible, but she did not see a counselor or share her anxieties with Bill. "You could call that pride, but I praise God we can depend on His Word and not other people, necessarily," she said in justification of her attitude. "To tell Bill would have been to burden him with a wife who was going to die."

Next Vonette went to Dr. Ralph Byron, a noted Christian surgeon at City of Hope Hospital in Duarte. He pronounced her fit as a fiddle. Then, when she told him about her premonition, Dr. Byron looked at her seriously and said: "Vonette, I don't believe that God does things like that. I don't believe He has told you you're going to die." (She had accepted the small interior voice as being from God.)

Vonette says she will always be grateful to Dr. Byron for not laughing at her when she told him about her fear.

Bill did laugh when she finally got up nerve to tell him nearly a year after the voice incident.

Bill said that he, too, had things like that happen to him all the time. "Vonette," he said, "this has to be an attack of the enemy to rob you of your security in Christ and to render you ineffective and keep you from being a strong witness."

Though this helped, her fears did not yet go away. And when Vonette lost her voice because of nodes on her vocal cords, she feared that for sure she had cancer of the throat.

A strong antibiotic apparently cleared up the problem and the nodes disappeared just in time for Bill and Vonette to leave for a scheduled trip to Japan.

"I felt it would be my last trip," Vonette said, wrinkling her nose. "Isn't it funny how your mind can play tricks on you?"

She survived the trip, and on June 30, 1960, just two years after she first heard the inner voice, she and Bill were on another trip, this time by car across country.

By then Vonette was able to joke about it somewhat. She turned to Bill. "This is supposed to be the last day of my life, sweetie. Drive carefully. But if I get through this day, I'll never be plagued by fear again."

HOW TO HANDLE FEAR

Vonette says now that while that was not fully true, she has learned how to handle fear. And, because she senses others are bothered by fears, too, Vonette has developed a Scripture study on fear and how God has provided the answer.

"We need have no fear of someone who perfectly loves us," she said, citing 1 John 4:18.

Through her death-fearing experience Vonette has learned to say, when bothered by a worry: "God, is this impression from You? If it is, You keep me anxious about it and impress to take action. If it is not of You, then take it away.

"More often than not, God takes the anxiety away," she says.

There is a difference between being fearful and being concerned, however, Vonette pointed out. Concern will take action; fear leads to frustration, criticism, and lack of trust: "To worry to the point of being plagued about something is really sin," Vonette feels.

Just as she did in overcoming the frustrations of housewife blahs, Vonette found the solution to fear in a changed attitude:

"The turning point was when I began to consider whether I was going to go through life fearing. And I prayed, 'God, if I can honor You more through my death than through my life, then I'm willing to die.'"

In the summer of 1976, God put the sincerity of that prayer to a tough test. Thirty-five women Campus Crusade leaders, including Vonette, were at a training retreat near Estes Park in the Rocky Mountains. In a sudden storm, the Big Thompson River overflowed it banks, flooding the entire canyon. The major disaster took the lives of seven Crusade women.

Vonette and eighteen of the girls became separated from the rest of the party during the confusion of evacuating the camp that stormy pitch-black night. In their search for higher ground, Vonette's party was taken to a vacant ranch building where they thought they would be safe for the rest of the night. They didn't know that only twenty yards away the raging Big Thompson was chafing at its banks.

The group bedded down on the floor, fitfully trying to sleep. "We trusted the rancher that we were in a safe place," recalled Vonette, remembering the nightmare of concern not only for their own safety but also for that of the rest who had been in the camp.

Vonette's party among them had one candle that wouldn't have burned long in the downpour and one flashlight. Still, one girl thought they ought to try to get out and find safer, higher ground. The girls turned to Vonette for leadership and guidance in the crisis.

"Let's pray that if we are in danger, God will keep us anxious," Vonette told them. "Let's pray that He will show us that we should get out of here and that He will give us a witness of the Spirit so we will know that's what

He wants. And if not, that He will give us confidence that our lives are safe and that we can trust Him that we should stay right here."

Vonette explained to me that she was applying the "sound mind principle," based on 2 Timothy 1:7 (KJV): "For God hath not given us the spirit of fear; but of power, and of love, and of a sound mind."

The rancher was familiar with the canyon and the river, she reasoned, he was reliable and rational, and he had guided them from where they had been in peril to safety thus far.

Vonette said she and the girls with her felt great peace and confidence in the decision not to leave the building during the night.

As dawn came, the women saw the destruction caused by the roaring flood waters and they carefully picked their way to higher ground by walking along a small ridge. They continued hiking to the crest of a mountain where, almost miraculously, they were met by Bill and a party of six or seven men who had been searching for them!

"If we recognize that God is a God of love, wisdom, sovereignty, and power then it's easy to be able to trust Him," Vonette nodded, reliving that traumatic night along the Big Thompson. "When we appropriate His power and draw from His resources then we can trust Him.

"But don't criticize yourself when you fail to be sitting on top of the world," she said, responding to my question about whether Christians should feel victorious all the time.

LIFE CONTROLLED BY GOD

Vonette added, "I believe Christians can live a life totally controlled by God. I see that kind of a walk with God in my husband's life and I'm getting there. This kind of abundant life is possible."

Four verses in the sixth chapter of the Book of Romans are especially helpful to Vonette in making that concept a reality: Verse 6, "know"; 11, "reckon"; 13, "yield," and 16, "obey."

"We *know* that our old self was crucified with Him so that the sinful body might be destroyed and we might no longer be enslaved to sin. So you also must *reckon* yourselves dead to sin and alive to God in Christ Jesus. Do not *yield* your members to sin as instruments of wickedness, but *yield* yourselves to God as men who have been brought from death to life, and your members to God as instruments of righteousness. Do you not know that if you yield yourselves to anyone as *obedient* slaves, you are slaves of the one you *obey*, either of sin, which leads to death, or of *obedience*, which leads to righteousness?"

"According to God's Word we are to *know* that we are crucified, buried and raised with Christ," Vonette explained, "and by faith we are to *reckon* this to be true in our daily walk with Christ. As an act of the will we are to *yield* to God our members, our attitudes, our actions to God, and then *obey* what He tells us to do."

Vonette also finds trusting God easier when she dwells on His attributes: "You learn you can have great confidence in Him when you fill your mind with the attributes of God: Sovereignty, love, holiness, righteousness, faithfulness, trustworthiness."

In her counseling, Vonette invites people to trust the Holy Spirit in three areas: to remove from their lives and cleanse anything not pleasing to Him; to empower them to cope with situations in the way most honoring to God; and to anoint them and perform in and through them whatever He wants them to do.

Vonette and I continued talking and sharing for another twenty minutes, though other responsibilities awaited both of us. The Brights have been special friends of mine through the years, beginning with my student days at UCLA when Campus Crusade was in its infancy.

"Is my brand of Christianity really worth sharing?" Vonette asked. Without waiting for an answer, she plunged on: "Man alive! One of the reasons why I'm so excited about sharing it is because it works. It's so practical. This is the only kind of life a person can live and really be above circumstances. It's the only way to find a total genuine peace of mind and solutions for the multitude of daily problems which face all of us."

Ann Kiemel

6

Changing Her World

"**Y**ou don't have to write a book. You don't have to stand on a platform. Just be all of God's wherever you are in your little square piece of the world. And keep that little square piece that only you and Jesus know about—keep that open and surrendered, and He will bless you."

That is Ann Kiemel speaking, a willowy, vivacious young lady who, with Jesus, has set out to change her world—and help others change theirs.

Still only thirty-two when she spoke these words at a church conference in Santa Maria, California, in the fall of 1977, Ann has come a long way in a very short time. But she gives the credit to Christ: "It has taken thousands of ordinary days of making Jesus Lord."

Born to a God-fearing small-town preacher and his wife, Ann has a twin sister and a brother. They were brought up in strict Nazarene tradition.

EARLY YEARS

Her early life and college experience were not remark-
able. But, in a God-directed path that took her from being
a schoolteacher in Kansas City to a job as youth director of
a turned-on and rapidly growing church in Long Beach
and then, at age twenty-six, to the position of dean of
women at Eastern Nazarene College near Boston, Ann
Kiemel has repeatedly demonstrated that God doesn't
know the word *impossible*.

Now she devotes all her time to crisscrossing the country speaking and writing, when she can squeeze it into a
sometimes exhausting schedule. Ann, in *I Love the Word
Impossible,* says in her own inimitable style:

> Impossible means that i
> an ordinary young woman,
> can be something special
> and significant in an enormous,
> hurting world.
> i can be love where i live,
> and that is Christ . . .
> and He really does make ALL the difference!

Her three books, each written in a kind of cross between poetic free verse (a style first made popular by the
late Peter Marshall), and first-person narrative, have tre-
mendously boosted Ann's popularity as a speaker at rallies, conventions, and conferences.

The first, *I'm Out to Change My World* (Impact Books),
was published in 1974, followed by *I Love the Word Impossible* and *It's Incredible* (both published by Tyndale
House), in 1976 and 1977, respectively.

"I became a Christian at age eight at a Billy Graham
movie *Oiltown U.S.A.,* just before the family moved to
Hawaii," Ann told me as we chatted in her hotel room in

Pasadena shortly before she addressed a luncheon meeting of thousands attending the Greater Los Angeles Sunday School Association convention.

"But that was before I came into a sense of my own personhood. I was a simple, uncomplicated, naive little girl. But when we moved to Hawaii I began to understand who Ann was. Ann was not a very exciting person in the eyes of the world. Being a twin made it difficult to find my identity, but it also gave me my best friend, so it was my salvation."

MINOR CRISES

And yet, if not seeming to be important was a minor crisis in Ann's early life, it also seems to be a struggle for her now that she has achieved wide recognition and admiration. One senses that she seeks it and basks in it, yet fears it and wants to subjugate it to her all-consuming passion to build around "the simple, central truth that Jesus is the ambition and fulfillment of my life."

And though Ann obviously enjoys knowing and being known by the superstars of the Christian evangelical world, she is able to say that some of the friends she treasures most are those the world has never heard about.

"These friends live in simple houses in simple neighborhoods, with big, wide, warm hearts. They know how to laugh and they know how to cry, and they know Jesus."

But back to Ann's growing-up years—the better to understand her maturing ones.

Her father's church in Hawaii was small, and the manse including the kitchen was part of the church. The Kiemels had to make financial sacrifices. For several years they did not even have enough money to buy a Christmas tree. And Ann felt the pressure of being one light face in the middle of several thousand dark faces on the campus.

She wished her skin were dark, too, and she wondered why the majority, Buddhists and Hindus, laughed at her Jesus.

A second trauma, of sorts, occurred when she left Hawaii for the mainland and college at Northwest Nazarene in Nampa, Idaho. Here, she says, she really committed her life to Jesus Christ. But, she wondered, "Could I cut it? Could I be accepted? Could I really find my place?"

She had big dreams, high hopes. She became *somebody* on campus. And she was an honor student.

Still, she writes in *I'm Out to Change My World,* what if her dreams never came true? Was she willing to follow Jesus even then—to the end?

> For you it might have been an easy decision.
>   For me it was six long months—
>   ugly months—
>   of struggle.
>   "Jesus, how can I?"
>   'Til I remember kneeling by the couch
>   in the TV room
>   and piling into my hands all that I loved and
>   knowing what it meant for the first time,
>   "Yes, Lord, from now to the end I will follow you."
>   Yes, Lord
>   to anything
>   anytime, anywhere.
>   Yes, Lord—if you'll go with me.

That, says Ann, really was the turning point in her life.

And so, not forgetting that lesson, poor, and far from her family, Ann went to Kansas City to teach school. She had dreamed of being on her own, yet suddenly, she recalls, she felt insecure as a somewhat shy teacher in a big, pseudosophisticated secular school.

She had never had a checking account, never rented an

apartment. But she found one: "One room, upstairs, no heat, no air conditioning, a bed that sagged, and a lamp stand."

Would Christ be adequate? "I was standing on my tiptoes, reaching for something higher than I'd ever reached before," said Ann in characteristic soft tones.

She continued talking, telling about subsequent moves, first to the church in Long Beach and then to Eastern Nazarene College in Wollaston, Massachusetts, where she was dean of women for five years. The great crises in her life have not been associated with moves, however.

NO PAT ANSWERS

"The overall great crisis," she explained, "was when I suddenly realized that truth isn't all black and white and that there aren't pat answers for everybody in the world. I was suddenly a woman, not a girl."

This process of revelation and resolution of internal truth happened when Ann was at Eastern Nazarene, "a young, young dean counseling all kinds of people and dealing with all the human emotions that there are."

Ann discovered she didn't always know what truth was, even for herself. Suddenly life wasn't pat. She was hearing many different voices telling her what was truth. And she realized she had never internalized what truth encompassed for her.

ABSOLUTE BELIEFS

Clarifying her thoughts, Ann added that she has never let loose of two absolute beliefs: One, that Jesus should be Lord of one's life; and two, that a person "should give his best—200 percent—to God every day—through ordinary days, unknown moments, the black tunnels, the rugged mountains."

But, she confided, it took her about six years to find "in the nitty gritty human experiences of life what is truth."

"I knew that if Jesus was Lord He would lead me into all this other truth," she said of her struggle. "But it didn't mean that He suddenly wrote on the walls about all the little human details of life.

"Today," she continued, "I believe I have internalized truth and understand what I'm going to live and die by in a deeper way than ever before and what it means to make Jesus sovereign Lord of a person's life.

"I believe life is one big process that involves pain and stretching and testing—a process that can only be discovered sometimes by testing, trials and failures. But the 'Spirit of Truth will lead us into all truth.' (*See* John 16:13.) Our only hope for positive process is Christ, at work in our lives. Without Christ at the center, the process will be distorted and will distort us."

SHE TURNS TO PRAYER

When Ann is searching for truth and answers for her life, she turns to prayer with a genuine earnest heart.

"The Lord has said that if you seek Him you will find Him when you search with all your heart," she said, referring to Jeremiah 29:13.

She also turns to Christian writings for guidance, especially the works of Oswald Chambers, E. Stanley Jones, and Catherine Marshall.

Also, close friends "who will love you through everything" are an important source of spiritual help in times of distress, as well as an aid in coping with life's day-to-day needs.

"Find one or two people you utterly trust who will not betray you, to whom you can open your whole life and stand naked and bare before," Ann advises. "Those who will believe in you, pick you up over and over, dust you off, and identify with you in your struggle."

Admittedly, she feels, few friends are of that quality who will share your private sanctuary with you. Ann, who greatly admires her parents, nonetheless says parents can't be that kind of sanctuary to a child though they can be of great help in many other ways.

To Ann, at least, a sibling can provide the kind of friendship that incorporates totality and trust. Ann calls her twin sister Jan, "my greatest, noblest friend. If I hadn't had Jan I wouldn't be where I am today. It's taken Jesus and Jan."

Another nuance to friendships and interpersonal relationships is a source of spiritual strength, Ann feels. Commitment to others is as important to her as having a few very significant persons whom she can trust.

COMMITMENT TO OTHERS

"It goes back to the idea of seed faith," she explained when she realized I didn't quite understand her. "It's not losing touch with the fact that there are people around you, and being committed to these people and to a cause greater and higher than yourself."

Put in another context, this giving of oneself to others can be a means of letting God revive one's own drooping spirits.

Ann, like nearly all of those interviewed for this book, is subject to periods of discouragement—sometimes, to use her own words, she is "deeply, deeply discouraged. I awake feeling disjointed with life. There are a few mornings when it would have been easier to have never gotten out of bed."

That is a frank admission from a gal who, in public appearances at least, seems to be sitting on top of the world.

But the average Christian needs to know that even their best models in the faith sometimes feel like Ann: "With sheer gut determination I got out of bed, got my clothes on, and began to bring laughter, cheer, and hope to others around me."

I asked her if she ever felt hypocritical about this when her true feelings underneath were at variance with those she was conveying from the stool she likes to sit on while speaking to a crowd.

Ann has never felt hypocritical about this: "I feel that God understands my heart and knows that I really want to give it my best," she answered. "I am human and I am struggling. Besides, I only speak of things I really believe. Jesus will move people through other everyday people like me. And love changes everything."

What do you do then about *down times?* I asked.

ON TOP THROUGH CHRIST

The love of Christ has brought her out on top, through His faithfulness, "over and over and over and over again," she replied emphatically, "through loss and gain, sickness and health, success and failure, easy times and rough times. It's easier now because I know who He is and how faithful He is. How consistent He is in His love! It's not quite as much of a wilderness now."

Ann takes a realistic attitude towards discouragement and problems people, seeking help, bring to her. She doesn't try to talk them out of their problems, says the former dean of women.

"I think it's part of life. It's understanding, it's listening, it's saying, 'I care. Maybe I can't take the pain out of your life but I'll walk the road with you. I love you, care for you, believe in you.' "

Her books abound with examples of how she has tried to put that philosophy and counseling technique into practice.

GIVE GOD TIME

The single most important lesson she has learned, Ann asserted, can be told in three words: "Give God time."

The problem is, she said, we want everything NOW, without pain or struggle. "We want Christ to create this utopian, euphoric existence so it will just sort of fall into place."

Of course that's impossible. "It may take years of ordinary days and mistakes, thinking, learning. We need a resilient spirit, striving on toward Jesus' plan for us."

In her early thirties, Ann seems to have learned a lesson many twice her age have not yet mastered: "Let Jesus be the top priority of your life, day by day; everything else will fall into place, even though it may take years."

Ann pointed out that her father, who has always been the pastor of small churches, has given Jesus the best of his life each day. Nowadays he's being fulfilled through his children in some ways that were never possible in his own ministry. Vicariously he can share in the joy of speaking to vast audiences through Ann.

"Making Jesus Lord, one day at a time," summarized Ann, "takes hard work, initiative, determination, great courage, and positive energy.

"It takes everything Christ can put into my life and my best efforts. It's a combination of both. It's not passive, but it's surrendered and relaxed. It's inner freedom, serenity, inner peace, inner continuity."

MEETING DAILY ANXIETIES

Yes, and there are daily anxieties. The best time to deal with them, according to the lithe brunette who enjoys tennis, bicycling, and baking cookies, is before getting out of bed in the morning. Her first waking thought is to "acknowledge God's presence in my life—that He is Lord—and give Him the day."

There is also anxiety reduction in detachment. It is important, Ann believes, to detach oneself from the superficial securities of the world and what's going to make her happy, look good, be a success, impress people.

"I detach myself from thinking the way the world thinks, from success, money, how many people love me or don't love me. I want to build my life around Jesus as the ambition and fulfillment of all my desires and dreams and my personhood."

Admitting this is easier to do some days than others, Ann added: "I sometimes have to get back to that. There are moments of feeling insecure, threatened, alone, uncertain, and frightened. Then I need to go back to Jesus, the source of security, for my fulfillment. That is all that really matters."

To start and work through the day with these internalized convictions, many Christians would agree, is a big step towards driving away unhealthy stress and anxiety.

Because Ann Kiemel (at least when I interviewed her) was the only subject of this book who had never been married, I asked her to comment about singleness, anxiety, and living a life of victory in Christ.

Ann began by saying that as a little girl she had always wanted to be a wife and mother. Now, she insists, she is happy as a single.

"I am fulfilled today because I find Christ is more and more fulfilling if you let Him," she said simply.

Sure she gets lonely. Read her books and you get the feeling that at times she fairly aches with loneliness. But not to the point of devastation.

Especially hard, she remarked, are vacation times when she goes off alone. Her brother and sister are both married, and Ann says it isn't her bag to go off with a group of women. She would enjoy a trip with a man she likes. But that is not an option. So she spends time by herself.

Singles also feel the void of loneliness in the area of having to make big decisions alone.

But, she shrugged, everyone has periods of loneliness, regardless of marital or family status.

GIVE YOUR LIFE AWAY

"If I'd give one piece of advice to singles," Ann said after a pause—realizing that four out of the five of us in the room were single—"it's give your life away. Don't spend all your time sitting around with other singles moping and discussing how hard it is to be single.

"Stand up, move out. Wherever there is a need, fill it; a hurt, touch it in His name; loneliness around you, reach out to ease it. Give your life away."

Many singles, Ann feels, have very small worlds because they are looking for something God hasn't chosen to give them yet. If they would plant seeds, touch others, and give life away, then God could create bigger worlds for them, and the more whole they would feel.

One of Ann's goals is to be "self-contained, fulfilled, and whole." That is dependent upon Jesus being her source, she believes, not upon a relationship to a man.

"Forget about yourself and concentrate on Him," Ann advised. "Nothing will be more fulfilling than Jesus— even if you do marry and have children. If I marry, I'll be so much more and have so much more to offer as a woman because of the years I've been single, discovering truth, learning to be self-contained, and being independent. God has used that in my life."

In less than forty minutes now, Ann would have to change clothes, collect her thoughts for her message to the Sunday-school convention, and meet scores of friends and admirers eager to shake her hand, exchange a word of greeting or encouragement, and perhaps get her to autograph a copy of her latest book.

"Whatever I've been in the past is not good enough for today," Ann said. "He expects new, fresh courage for life each day. I can't live on my victories of the past in the world's eyes, either. The motive has to be pure. I must decrease and He increase."

Even as the titles of her best-selling books proclaim,

Ann's credo is that life and the potential of one's life are so great and expansive they are limitless.

She speaks with the same airy artistry of metaphors with which she writes. Her closing words:

> "I have miles and miles to go
> and dreams and dreams
>   to reach for
> and many mountain peaks to attain
>   through His power.
>   That is the adventure
> and the challenge
>   of my life."

Maria Von Trapp

7

Yielded Novice

The Mother Superior of a Benedictine Abbey in Austria called in a young novice. The pretty girl, with twinkling eyes, was a trifle worried about the reason for her summons; she was often in minor trouble for her independent, sometimes mischievous ways.

"How much have you learned while you've been here? What is the most important thing in life?" the Catholic nun demanded sharply.

Maria Von Trapp, hoping that she wasn't going to be reprimanded for some violation, replied without hesitation: "To find the will of God and then go and do it."

"Even if it is hard?" asked the Mother Superior.

Maria answered quickly. "Of course, even if it is hard."

Maria Augusta Von Trapp was to become the heroine whose life has been portrayed in *The Sound of Music.* She and her family escaped from Austria during the takeover by Adolf Hitler and came to the United States in 1938. Mrs. Von Trapp, who has lived here ever since, now divides her time among writing, speaking engagements, and her duties as house mother at the Trapp Family Lodge in Stowe, Vermont.

But many events ordained by God have intervened between the present and that day when she, as a young novice, stood before the Mother Superior.

"Right then and there I was notified that a certain Navy captain, Baron Georg Von Trapp, had been asking for ten months for somebody to be a teacher for one of his seven children," Maria recapitulated as she refreshed my memory about her well-known life.

The nuns at the abbey had selected her for the job, and the Mother Superior had confirmed what would soon be known as well to Maria as truly the will of God for her life.

But at the moment, the news fell with a leaden sullenness.

"This was a great big cross to me," Maria recalled. "I didn't want to leave."

Still, her answer to the head of the abbey about finding the will of God and doing it was like a dowry that Maria took with her. For she fell in love with the baron's children—and the baron. They were soon married.

GO AND DO IT

"In that critical moment, it had proven to be the absolute right thing—to look for the will of God and then go and do it," Maria said during an interview at a national conference on charismatic renewal in Kansas City where she was speaking.

And that principle, which has been an abiding one throughout her life, was soon handed on to the Von Trapp children, who ranged in age from four to fourteen.

"Even the little ones caught on," Maria remembers. "I recall the youngest at age five talking to herself about whether she could go outside and play or whether she should stay inside and do her homework. With a resigned sigh, she said to herself that she knew it was right to do the homework first.

"Doing God's will became second nature in our whole family."

Turning to God for special guidance was also the key resource for the Von Trapp family when Hitler invaded Austria. At first, the Von Trapps tried to ignore the turmoil, hoping the storm would blow over. But it got worse. Details about the family's life are told in one of Mrs. Von Trapp's six books, *The Story of the Trapp Family Singers,* the true story on which three films and the musical *The Sound of Music* are based.

One day Baron Von Trapp called the family together and asked about finding the will of God. "Do we want to keep money and material goods?" he asked. "What about friends? What about spiritual things? What about honor and our faith?"

Within five minutes, Maria related, all opinions had been voiced and the family had made its decision. The children said they had to spy on other children at school, that they were constantly told what was wrong with the books they read and the friends with whom they associated.

WHERE THE WILL OF GOD WAS LEADING

"There was no question where the will of God was leading us," Maria said firmly. "We saw we could not stay." So they left, fleeing through a tunnel in the high Alps into Italy.

By this time the Von Trapps had nine and one-half children, Maria said with a smile.

Though the family had often sung together for entertainment both for themselves and others, they had never relied upon music as a livelihood. But now they were faced with the problem of earning enough money to live from day-to-day in a new country.

And once again the matter of finding God's will for their daily bread came into focus.

"The only thing we could do well together was sing, our family hobby," Maria noted. But her husband, a former Navy officer and a member of the nobility, passionately opposed putting the family on stage.

"God had to show us this was the only thing left," Maria recounted, adding that God's will often—at least at first—seems to be contradictory to what we would naturally infer.

And so, in the summer of 1937, before Hitler's troops swarmed in, the family assembled and asked: "What is the will of God in this situation?"

The question, honed to razor sharpness, was: "Is it morally wrong to present a concert for money?"

"We decided it was not," Maria said with the air of definiteness that characterizes many of her expressions. "This was the only way my husband, very much against his will, consented—because he felt it was God's will."

A concert in Salzburg was arranged during the special concert festival there by a famed opera singer, Lotte Lehmann. Because there were talent scouts in the audience, the Trapp Family Singers were on their way towards fame.

At first there were small parties and performances, with barely enough money to get through the day, according to Maria. Then the family's fame spread. A concert in Turin, where they had settled in the Alps in southern Tyrol, opened the gateway to the Italian opera circuit in Florence, Milan, and Rome.

"And concerts became our way of living for twenty years," summed up Maria. "God closed all of the other doors."

Singing for their own joy multiplied the joy, ultimately, of multiple millions of persons.

Expanding her comments about knowing the will of

God, Maria advised that when perceiving the Lord's direction seems hard, consider eliminating all but one thing, even if it seems so against your grain. "Then you are left with what God wants. And you set your teeth and with a big sigh, you do it.

"And if that choice truly is God's, then peace, security, and joy—not anguish and unhappiness—will follow," she said.

The singing Trapps traveled all over Europe, living very frugally in order to save money for their emigration to the United States.

When they finally arrived in 1938, it was "still under the will of God," according to Maria, who reiterated that the only important thing is to find the will of God, and that finding it is to know the kind of inner peace without which it is impossible for the Christian to live.

"Perhaps, however, the will of God is not always plain. What should a person do then?" I asked Maria.

GETTING IN TUNE WITH THE WILL OF GOD

"Start today. Begin right now," she responded. "Say in the morning, 'What does God want of me today?' Most of the time it is easy to find duties to do. People are waiting for us. But now and then you come to a crossroads."

Then, she believes, the charismatic experience of knowing the power and direction of the Holy Spirit can come to our aid.

"Ask the Holy Spirit to show you and help you," she advised. "Then it often becomes a process of elimination. The least popular thing is left, and that's the thing you go into."

For Maria, who is in her seventies, and for nearly all who try to follow God's leading, some days His will appears crystal clear. Other days it seems obscure.

On occasions when His guidance is wrapped in haze,

keep praying, says Maria. Pray, as Jesus and His mother, Mary, did, "Thy will be done."

A time for that kind of prayer came to Maria on the day her husband Georg died. "Then you can only say, 'Thy will be done,' " she said. "If you try to rebel, you end up saying, 'There can't be a God or He wouldn't have done this.' And you quarrel with God the rest of your life. This will undermine all your future happiness."

Maria, a devout Catholic, practices daily spiritual disciplines to keep spiritually fit.

First thing in the morning she has a heart-felt prayer. "I ask for guidance and offer up everything that will happen during the day as it comes," she explained. "I renew my will to do His will."

Most days she attends mass, for she receives strength through the Eucharist, she says.

Comparing the need for spiritual food to our bodily requirement of three meals a day, Maria said her spiritual diet consisted of going to mass, "spiritual reading"— books about other Christians and what they did to come closer to God—and a time for reading the Bible and praying.

SPIRITUAL DRYNESS

Maria did not speak about doubts or anxieties. But she did talk about the common problem Christians have of *spiritual dryness.* Most of it, she thinks, is the result of excuses: Too busy for mass or prayers.

When she travels through spiritual deserts, she tries to "talk it through with Jesus. I just plain sit it out."

Sometimes she takes her watch, sits down for fifteen minutes and concentrates on her need to pray and receive God's guidance.

She prays: "This time I promised to You and now I want my soul to listen to You, Jesus."

Because she is willing to discipline herself in this way,

it usually isn't long before the dry period passes, and Maria has, from God, "some splendid, good idea."

The devotional life, she feels, is an individual thing arising from the unique experiences of each person.

"Some say the rosary and have a devotion to Mary," she elaborated. "Others get great comfort from meditating on the Passion of Christ and the Stations of the Cross. For still others, devotion to the Sacred Heart is helpful if they have difficulty in daily loving. The heart of Jesus is a symbol of love."

The old tradition of each believer having a guardian angel is also a helpful concept for some people, Maria believes, for the idea of a spiritual being attached to a person to help him through life—if he turns to that help—is a source of security and comfort.

"Angels in communion with God are eager and so willing to help us," she said, adding, however, that helpful devotions are frowned on in some religious circles these days.

"But they will come back," she predicted. "The pendulum will swing to a middle point."

Maria, a sought-after speaker who always causes heads to turn wherever she is recognized because of *The Sound of Music,* believes that knowing the will of God is the same for everyone regardless of circumstances or station in life.

"When we come out of our various concentration camps, we are on the same level again," she said, indicating that World War II experiences are still very much a part of her memories. "Then comes the everyday battle, which we face day after day. Sometimes it is easier to face the big battles like the concentration camps than it is to face the tedium of everyday battles."

Quoting from her German Bible, Maria paraphrased from Revelation 2:10: "Whoever keeps up to the end will be given the crown of life eternal."

"It's the everyday keeping up," she nodded. "It is a continuing struggle—and also a joy.

"Life is not a constant joy for anyone," she continued in her noticeable but not distracting German accent. "First and foremost, it wasn't for our Lord. He had to struggle every day.

"There is a long, long exercise in bearing a daily cross. There is still a yoke and a burden, but He makes it easier."

D. Elton Trueblood

8

Thoughtful Quaker

"I'm beautifully emancipated, freed, unemployed. I say to you, get sixty-five as fast as you can. It gives you freedom to do what you think you ought to do."

With these words, D. Elton Trueblood welcomed me into his square, red-brick study lined with walnut paneling. It was a pleasant Sunday afternoon, and Trueblood, dressed in a sportshirt, was cheerful and optimistic as he showed me about the study, where he has a library of 2,000 books—and no typewriter. The building is about 100 feet from the Truebloods' attractive home on the edge of the Earlham College campus, a small Quaker school in Richmond, Indiana.

On the way from the parking lot to Trueblood's study I had already noticed his carefully laid-out vegetable garden and the manicured rose bushes lining the walkway. Above the walk, suspended from a branch of a 250-year-old white oak tree, hung a wooden yoke symbolizing

Yokefellows International, a Christian fellowship of discipline founded by Trueblood in 1952.

YOKEFELLOWS

Yokefellows was one of Trueblood's works that took shape in embryo form at Stanford but came to fruition at Earlham. It has flourished on an international scale. During 1946–47, his first year at Earlham, a group of students who held to the idea of a small, covenanted fellowship that took on a voluntary discipline, something like a Christian order, met with Trueblood. As yet the fellowship had no name. Two years later, however, the group was using the yoke metaphor and the name *Yokefellow* emerged. It is used in Philippians 4:3 as a synonym for a practicing Christian.

The movement has grown to include five retreat houses and a modest headquarters office next to Trueblood's study and home at 230 College Avenue, Richmond, Indiana 47374.

The common discipline voluntarily undertaken by Yokefellows contains seven points: daily prayer, daily Bible reading, weekly public worship, systematic giving for Christian causes, wise use of time, making daily work a Christian vocation, and productive study habits.

"We can now see that much of the success of the Yokefellow movement has arisen from the fact that, when it began, it represented an early form of the New Evangelicalism," Trueblood wrote his Yokefellow partners at Christmastime 1977.

"For twenty-five years we have been stressing commitment as the central Christian experience. We have said, in season and out of season, that it is not necessary to choose between a Christ-centered faith and either intellectual integrity or devotion to the cause of justice, but we have always held that commitment to Christ is the place to start. With that as a beginning, both intellect and justice may be served . . . ."

LIFE LIVED IN CHAPTERS

Trueblood's happiness in taking retirement at sixty-five in 1966 fits in perfectly with his philosophy that life is lived best when it is lived in chapters. And the chapter he was living during the summer of 1977 when I visited him is perhaps the most rewarding of his long and influential career.

In 1970, Trueblood taught his last class in college. On July 6, 1973, he gave his last lecture at a pastors' school. After writing several hundred editorials and columns, he phased out that kind of journalism in June 1973. His final book—his thirty-first—was published in 1974, thirty-nine years after his first one, *The Essence of Spiritual Religion*. Harper & Row published the first and the last—his autobiography *While It Is Day*—and most of the other volumes in between. And November 13, 1977, was the date of Trueblood's last speaking engagement.

Not that the eighth-generation Quaker with English roots traded a busy life for a rocking chair. Nor was his health failing. In fact, he told me he had never been a patient in a hospital.

"Though any particular finality is sobering," Trueblood wrote in the last chapter of his autobiography, "it need not be sad. Certainly it is not sad if each ending provides for new beginnings. It is in this spirit that I face the remaining years of my life, in which the conclusion of certain experiences merely opens the way to the enjoyment of others."

The title of Trueblood's autobiography *While It Is Day* is a phrase from Jesus' words to the disciples when He healed a blind man: "We must work the works of him who sent me, while it is day; night comes, when no one can work" (John 9:4 RSV). Although Trueblood, who lives with his second wife Virginia finds there is really nothing wrong with "sitting on the terrace just being quietly thankful," he keeps busy with the Yokefellows and with a new kind of writing ministry.

"Since I'm not writing any more books, I'm helping others with theirs," he told me, showing me a manuscript he had recently received in the mail. "I get about one a week—all unsolicited." Advice and editing from the veteran author don't cost the neophyte writers a penny.

In harmony with his orderly life-style, Trueblood, who every night puts his watch on the bedroom dresser and goes to bed at precisely 10:00 P.M., has divided his life into eight chapters, or segments: child, student, teacher, author, minister, yokefellow, father, and rambler.

CRISIS OF FAITH

The minister chapter is the period when major changes occurred. In a sense, it was a crisis of faith. The famed British author C. S. Lewis was instrumental in shaping Trueblood's shifting theology.

In the early days of his ministry, Trueblood emphasized the compassion and humanness of Jesus but said little of His teachings about Himself or His unique relationship to God the Father. Slowly and subtly, however, the influences of C. S. Lewis began to seep in.

"He shocked me out of my unexamined liberalism and into evangelicalism," Trueblood, who holds a Doctor of Philosophy degree from Johns Hopkins University, explained. "Jesus claimed to be more than a teacher—that's the heart of it."

For Trueblood, like T. S. Eliot, full commitment came through the intellect, though he has strongly felt that the inner life of devotion and the outer life of service are also needed for a full-orbed Christian faith.

"In reading Lewis I could not escape the conclusion that the popular view of Christ as being a teacher, and *only* a teacher, has within it a self-contradiction that cannot be resolved," Trueblood notes in *While It Is Day*. "I saw, in short, that conventional liberalism cannot survive rigorous and rational analysis. What Lewis and a few others

made me face was the hard fact that if Christ was only a
teacher, then He was a false one, since, in His teaching,
He claimed to be *more.*"

One day, Trueblood suddenly realized that, without
intending to be, he was an evangelical.

RATIONAL ANSWERS

New confidence in Christ gave Trueblood rational answers to some important questions that had been nagging
him. His preaching took on new confidence, too, because
he realized that the trustworthiness of Christ was his one
central certainty.

"When I found that thoughtful people would listen to a
Christ-centered approach, I realized where the power of
the Christian faith resides," he wrote in his autobiography. "While many churches are declining in strength,
the churches which exhibit both Christ-centeredness and
rationality are marked by evident vitality."

Writing more on the subject in the December 1977
"Quarterly Yoke Letter," sent to persons interested in the
work of the Yokefellows, Trueblood said:

"The evangelical rejects 'religion in general,' which he
recognizes as powerless, just as he rejects any faith which
is merely formal or external. His religion is one of *power*
because he has experienced the reality of Christ in his
own inner life. The evangelical Christian, as a direct result
of commitment to Christ, being yoked with Him, and
consequently with his fellow Christians, is no longer a
mere 'church goer.' He is liberated from the dullness
which has afflicted much of the religion of the recent
past . . . .

"Those who begin with the conviction of the Christlikeness of God still have many problems and they are not
free from burdens," continued Trueblood, "but they
normally achieve, by means of the concreteness of their
faith, a stability that is truly amazing."

TIMES OF DECISION

Times of decision have not been taken lightly by True-blood, despite his easygoing manner. Career choices have included five professorships: Guilford, Haverford, Harvard, Stanford, and Earlham. The decision to leave Stanford in 1945 after more than nine years as chaplain and professor of the philosophy of religion was especially difficult.

"I decided to leave a great, rich, glittering university to come to a small, midwestern Christian college," Trueblood said. He went through inner turmoil over the matter and could have stayed on at Stanford with ease. Still, the tone of his voice told me Trueblood had no regrets about his choice.

Soon he found himself equally at home—perhaps more so—at Earlham, and he wrote a widely circulated article for *Reader's Digest* called "Why I Chose a Small College."

"Besides," he said, "I would never have started the Yokefellow movement if I hadn't come to Earlham."

"How did God help you to decide between Stanford and Earlham?" I asked.

"I said to myself," Elton replied, "He has made me one person in His image and given me this life. He has not coerced me. He has given me the chance to make mistakes, and to choose."

In a mood of prayer, not merely on his own power, Trueblood concluded that since he had been given only one earthly life, he had better not miss the chance to use his talents at the small Quaker school.

Trueblood feels a keen sense of responsibility for the right use of the powers God has given him and for the importance of finding the natural divisions of life. Part of this concept he gleaned from Robert Frost's poem, "The Road Taken." The metaphor of life as a journey was appealing to Trueblood, who declared that the consequences of decisions along the way are beyond knowing except by faith.

DEMAND FOR SPIRITUAL RESOURCES

The lengthy illness and subsequent death of Elton's first wife, Pauline, was an episode in the author-professor's life that demanded great dependence upon the spiritual resources of the Lord.

Always of rather frail health, yet the mother of three sons and a daughter, Pauline came under the shadow of progressive illness in 1954. Within six months she was paralyzed and died of brain cancer at the age of fifty-three. It was a difficult time, especially for the children. The youngest was only thirteen. The family had been a close one.

At the time Pauline passed on, Elton turned to his beliefs about the nature of God. "I was convinced that God *is*, that He is like Jesus Christ, and that not a sparrow falls without His knowledge," he said as we sat in his book-lined study near a photograph of Abraham Lincoln.

"My task, therefore, was to go on and perform the ministry to which I was devoted."

To Trueblood, this meant giving a promised talk in Cincinnati in the evening of the day Pauline died. "I had made the commitment; I thought the honorable thing was to keep the promise," he said simply.

And he quoted from Dr. Samuel Johnson of England, one of his favorite models and men of faith, about the sacredness of time—a quotation Johnson had inscribed on his watch. Trueblood has read Johnson's books nearly every week for forty years and has written two books of his own on Johnson's prayers.

"We're here a little while, and we better use time well . . . I'm going to use every moment well; I'm going to use every day I've got."

Intuitively—or perhaps through prayer—Trueblood has

seemed to sense the passing of one chapter of his life and the beginning of the next. The day I interviewed him in Richmond he had decided it was time to resign from the board of Catalyst, a cassette tape ministry for ministers.

"I think the Lord is leading me to stay put and let people come to me," said the man who had averaged one book and 250 speeches every year for the previous thirty. His moratorium on book-writing didn't extend to hymns, however. He had just completed "New Pentecost," a hymn for contemporary Christians to be sung to the tune of St. Anne, perhaps the best-known hymn tune in the modern world. It is usually associated with the words to "Our God Our Help in Ages Past."

Trueblood believes in *the guiding Hand* for spiritual help. And, as a Quaker affiliated with the Friends United Meeting, he thinks Christians should spend more time in silence listening to God and less time doing all the talking.

He prays for friends, family, and associates by name each morning. Then he waits and listens. A prayer group meets with Trueblood at Earlham five days a week.

Trueblood, who calls himself utterly ecumenical, believes you can't be a Christian alone. Group guidance is essential, too. "There is individual listening and there is group guidance," he said to me. "In short, my friend, we need all the help we can get and we need to get it from every valid source."

DOUBTS, NOT ANXIETIES

Trueblood, who holds honorary doctoral degrees from twelve institutions of higher learning, said he is conscious of intellectual doubts in his life—but not anxieties. In this regard, his response corresponded with that of another professor-theologian: Carl F. H. Henry, whose own chapter is in this book.

"God has not, in our finitude, given us absolute certainty about anything," explained Trueblood. "The Christian life is one of trust, always shadowed by doubt."

In fact, Trueblood sees philosophic doubt as beneficial, not just unavoidable. "It keeps us humble," he said with a smile. "Watch out for the fellow who is too sure."

We are not to expect certainty, according to Trueblood. That's why we live by faith, and not by an absolute sense of being right.

Still, though a person never has absolute certainty, he can see that the evidence that this is God's world is stronger than the evidence that it is not.

GOD IS

Christ turns the balance, Trueblood is convinced, and his logic is sharp and clear: Either God is, or Christ is wrong. "If Christ is trustworthy, then God is, because Christ believed in Him and prayed to Him," Trueblood reasons. Much of Trueblood's philosophical and theological apologetics are contained in what he calls his most enduring book, *A Place to Stand* (Harper & Row, 1969).

"Nearly everything I know about God, I know through Christ," Trueblood continued. "I go from the known to the unknown—not the other way around from God to Christ."

Trueblood elucidated that his knowledge of Christ comes from two sources. One is the Gospels, through which we are able to learn something of what Jesus did and said and that He died and rose. The other is immediate, first-hand, personal knowledge.

"I sense His presence in the midst," said Trueblood, employing a Quaker expression.

Though he is not given to anxieties, Trueblood thinks moods are a normal part of being alive and human. "The reality is not on cloud nine, it's right here," he said, pointing to the ground. "The person who says 'nothing ever worries me' I know is a nut!"

Idealism that isn't realistic drives people crazy in True-blood's estimation, because it is almost sure to make them live falsely.

But Christ, far from being an idealist, is "a theistic realist," he added, borrowing a phrase from the late Scottish theologian Dr. John Baillie, an erstwhile friend of both Trueblood and myself.

"It's entirely possible," summed up the dean of American religious writing, " to have the warm heart and the clear head. You don't have to choose—praise God!"

Walter Hoving

9

He Tries God

The tall, spare, silver-haired executive was stranded, like thousands of others caught in the crippling power blackout in New York City in July 1977.

He couldn't get into his apartment at River House, a fancy complex for the elite. The elevators weren't running. And he couldn't even use a stairway because the emergency exit doors had no knobs on the outside.

So Walter Hoving, chairman of the board and chief executive of Tiffany & Co., spent the night curled on the Lawson sofa in his sixth-floor paneled office in the famed jewelry store at Fifth Avenue and Fifty-seventh Street. He rested his head on the blue pillow, embroidered in gold thread with the words TRY GOD, that his daughter had made.

But he turned over the pillow so the words faced down.

"I didn't think I should be sleeping on God," said Hoving, a soft-spoken man but one who nevertheless has strong convictions. He added, with a smile, during an interview in the Tiffany board room: "People without a sense of humor have difficulty finding God."

The innovative merchandiser and devout Episcopalian not only found God in a personal way many years ago, he also is encouraging thousands of others to try Him, too, through Jesus Christ.

"TRY GOD" PIN

Though he may have turned over the TRY GOD pillow that his daughter, Petie, made him, his TRY GOD pins and pendants—registered Tiffany trademarks and sold only by the prestigious firm—have turned over a sparkling profit for the Walter Hoving Home for troubled girls at Garrison, near West Point in New York. In the first two years after ads appeared in major newspapers, forty-seven thousand of the TRY GOD pins had sold at Tiffany's six stores. Proceeds of $367 thousand were turned over to the home.

The sterling pins and pendants sell for ten dollars. The fourteen-karat version is twenty-five dollars, still a bargain at a store that displays the $7 million canary diamond and where "moderately priced" jewelry begins at two thousand to three thousand dollars, and inexpensive jewelry begins at one hundred dollars.

The success of the TRY GOD campaign has been greatly boosted by evangelist Billy Graham, who purchased at cost and gave away nearly 600 thousand additional pins through his religious broadcasts.

Hoving, who has passed the eighty-year mark, is firmly convinced that not only the Hoving Home, but Tiffany's itself—which did $60 million in business in 1977—is "run by the Lord."

To Hoving, the Sweden-born son of a Finnish cardiologist and a Danish opera singer, the Christian faith is simple, and he adds, "Jesus works in business life as in every other area."

None who knows Hoving or his works can doubt the sincerity of that belief nor its apparent success at the practical level.

Hoving points with pride to what is claimed to be the 94 percent cure ratio for girls who stay at the Walter Hoving Home for the twelve months required to graduate.

"We don't cure the heroin habit, we change the person, through God," Hoving explained, adding that nine out of ten of the girls who stay a year are still free of drugs three years or longer after they leave. A book, *Try God* by Laura Hobe and published by Doubleday, tells in detail the dramatic story of the home and about the lives of five young women who found release there from drugs, alcohol, and delinquency.

The Reverend David Wilkerson, who founded Teen Challenge, the nationwide ministry to youth, was cofounder of Hoving Home. "This," he says of the home, "is the story of God's love reaching out to change lives, from the glitter of Tiffany's to the gutter of rebellion and addiction. Girls who have been given up by society become powerful missionaries and love-channels of God's mercy."

The home, about an hour's drive from Manhattan, was opened in the summer of 1967 and is managed by John W. Benton. It now cares for fifty-four young women, ages eleven through thirty. The home was purchased when Hoving referred its managers to a foundation which bought the property, but it is always short of funds.

The idea for the TRY GOD pin came from Eleanor McManus, a member of a small witness group that Hoving leads every Thursday evening at Saint Bartholomew's Episcopal Church.

When people who complained of their troubles and problems asked her advice, she invariably would tell them, "Why don't you try God?" In a moment of excitement at one of the Thursday-night prayer meetings, Mrs.

McManus asked Tiffany's chairman, "Could your store design a pin with just the words, 'Try God'?"

Hoving returned to Tiffany's the next morning and the creation of the simply styled TRY GOD pin began. But Hoving knew it was impossible to make just one pin for her at reasonable cost. Soon he hit on the plan to produce thousands, turning over the profit to the financially ailing Hoving Home.

Under a photograph of the pin, the first ad read: "This is a limited edition; that is, limited to people who believe in God." The response was a deluge of orders.

SUCCESS CAME NATURALLY

Success has always seemed to come naturally to the gentlemanly and proper Hoving, though it took a span of years before he became aware of the power and influence of God in his business as well as his professional life.

His terse biography, which he has confined to one single-spaced sheet, outlines the measure of a man who has reached the top of this world's achievement ladder.

A graduate of Brown University in 1920, Walter Hoving was formerly a vice-president of R. H. Macy & Co., vice-president of Montgomery Ward, president of Lord & Taylor, and president of Bonwit Teller. While heading Lord & Taylor, he initiated the Lord & Taylor American Design Awards to encourage original design in the United States.

The founder of the Salvation Army Association of New York and its president for twenty years, Hoving was awarded the Salvation Army Distinguished Service Cross. He also was a founder of the United Negro College Fund and a founder of the USO (United Services Organization) and its first president, as well as being chairman of the USO National Board during World War II.

Add these accomplishments: president of the Fifth Avenue Association, the National Institute of Social Sci-

ences, the Commerce and Industry Association of New
York, and a trustee of Brown University.

He has been senior warden of Saint Bartholomew's
Church in New York and is now an honorary warden
there. And in 1974 the Religious Heritage of America
honored him with its Churchman of the Year Award. The
same year, the American Assembly of Collegiate Schools
of Business gave him the first annual Dow Jones Award
after he sponsored the Tiffany Lecture Series on Corporate
Design Management at the Wharton School at the University of Pennsylvania. The award was given to recognize
his outstanding contribution to the field of collegiate education for business and administration.

Yet, it wasn't until 1946—when Hoving, president at
the time of Lord & Taylor, quit that $135,000-a-year job to
buy Bonwit Teller—that he found true happiness. Although active in religious activities of many kinds, it took
what he calls the first real shocker to convince him that
Christianity isn't a religion but rather a personal relationship to Jesus Christ.

Crossing his long legs as he sat in Tiffany's board room
during an interview with me in late July 1977, Hoving,
dressed impeccably in a conservatively tailored gray
business suit, recalled the struggle to scrape together the
cash to buy out Bonwit Teller. He had put up half a million of his own money. But another $2.5 million was
needed for the down payment. Walter left his office about
noon on a Saturday in June 1946. He walked up bustling
Fifth Avenue intending to visit an art exhibit.

AN INNER VOICE

"I distinctly heard an inner voice say, 'Go home and
telephone,' " Hoving remembers. "I really felt it was the
Lord speaking to me. I never had heard anything like it
before."

The executive did as the inner voice directed. He

needed to obtain financing from a maximum of twenty-five people, according to Security and Exchange Commission regulations. He dialed and talked all the rest of Saturday and all day Sunday.

The deal had to close by Tuesday afternoon at 2:00 P.M. By Monday morning Hoving still lacked $800 thousand of his $2.5 million goal for the Bonwit Teller down payment.

Monday, however, brought a call to Hoving from an officer of the Massachusetts Investors Trust. He offered to buy the remaining $800 thousand in the forming corporation.

"And we closed the deal on that Tuesday at 2:30 P.M.," Hoving recalls happily.

The episode touched Hoving with more than money. "This made me very conscious that something was going on that I hadn't realized," he said. "Little things had been happening that Jesus was doing, but I hadn't known it at the time. You have to get yourself out of the way, open yourself up, and let Jesus in.

"That's the absolute cardinal principle. Everything else is subordinate. He is very anxious to come in, more anxious to help than you are to ask His help. He stands at the door and knocks."

Those little things that Walter Hoving said had been happening in his life—the same kind of proddings and guidance that all Christians may feel at times—actually dated back to 1929. But he says he didn't catch on at the time.

Again, it was a financial transaction when he was a vice-president at R. H. Macy Company—that time involving Macy's stock. Another man in the company was willing to lend him, interest free, the $98 thousand Hoving needed for broker's fees. But Hoving turned him down. In retrospect, he believes, "Jesus was telling me not to accept it. I know now the Lord did not want me to make money. He wanted me to hang on, to trust Him, but I didn't get the message at the time."

Of course, Hoving didn't know at the time, either, that the stock market was soon to crash. He was able to sell the stock which he had bought and come out exactly even. Stock he had bought at $195 a share eventually dropped to $3 a share in the Depression.

Hoving also thinks God's hand was staying him from becoming in debt to the executive at Macy's. For when an offer came to Hoving to become vice-president of Montgomery Ward's at three times his Macy's salary, he took it. "But I don't think I would have if I still owed [Percy] Strauss ninety-eight thousand dollars," Hoving reflected. "I would have felt an obligation to stay at Macy's."

He added that he had no way to foresee or accomplish what was done: "I could have gotten head over heels in debt, but I came out even. My life was completely changed by the Lord, though I didn't know it at the time. But then, in 1946, when I again felt God's nudges in the buying of Bonwit Teller, I could see what the Lord had done for me."

GOD'S GUIDANCE

In 1961 Hoving once again saw God's guidance in business life as in every other way. By then, however, he was, as he described himself, a practicing, praying Christian.

This time Hoving was attempting to put together a deal for a controlling interest in Tiffany's. He thought a certain man was going to go in on $1 million in stock, but two days before the closing date, the man was nowhere to be found.

"There I was, sitting at the Irving Bank, waiting for the noon closing, short a million dollars!" Hoving anguished as he relived the moments of anxiety. "I finally got the man on the phone and he agreed to go to Wall Street and borrow the million."

But at 11:45 A.M. the man called Walter and said, "I can't get the money!"

"It got to be 12 o'clock—12:05—12:10—and then one of the bank vice-presidents came in and said, 'Walter, for goodness sakes, everybody's waiting for you, what's the matter?' "

" 'Well, I'm short a million,' I said."

Five minutes later another man appeared with a million dollars, without requiring collateral, to lend to Hoving.

"That's how we closed that one," chuckled Hoving. "The Lord did that; there's no way I could have influenced any of those events."

Walter Hoving is a complex man, with a shrewd business sense. He has the grace of a British peer coupled with firm ideas about what constitutes good design, manners, morals, and aesthetic elegance. But his faith is quintessentially simple. He says he doesn't have times of doubting or anxieties.

"Before time was, God was," he says. "God's first decision was to create the human race. Then He had to create everything for the human race to be. He created time and electromagnetism, out of which He created matter." The function of the planets and stars, he believes, is to keep the earth 93 million miles from the sun—the exact distance to keep us from either burning up or freezing.

And the seasons? "Scientists don't know how the seasons were created. The Lord tipped the earth. Nobody but God could have thought up such a simple thing."

"The moon is 235 thousand miles from the earth, just the right distance to cause the right tides in the oceans. "God banged the moon with meteors to drive it just that far away."

To Hoving, it is ridiculous and stupid not to think of God as the Creator and Sustainer: "It is so clear to me that the Lord runs everything."

It is also crystal clear to him that Christian faith is a personal relationship with God. "The whole thing is when you feel you have a personal relationship and He leads you in things you couldn't have believed possible," he explains. "When the Lord does things for you, the ego becomes tinged with a great deal of humility."

But the problem, as he sees it, is the confusion that has been made between religion as an organization or system of belief and a faith relationship.

CHRISTIANITY IS A FAITH

"Christianity is not a religion, it's a faith," he said to me during the first moments of our Tiffany's interview. He was to repeat that thought from different perspectives throughout our visit.

"The worst mistake was when Constantine the Great declared Christianity a state religion in A.D. 325. It acquired the trappings and the hierarchy of a religion; Christianity is therefore classed along with all the other religions."

The big fallacy, Hoving firmly believes, is that Adam's sin was that he tried to play God. "That's original sin. All this stuff about being the captain of one's soul means playing God. People hate to give that up. This is a very difficult thing."

"Behold, I stand at the door, and knock: if any man hear my voice, and open the door, I will come in to him, and will sup with him, and he with me" (Revelation 3:20 KJV). Quoting this verse, he observed: "This has kind of been lost. You have to open yourself to Him."

Walter Hoving tries to open himself up to God every day. I asked him what spiritual resources he uses in moments of decision and crisis, as well as for everyday strength to cope.

Prayer, he replied without a moment's hesitation, is the sine qua non of the spiritual life.

"I say, 'Thank You, God, for little things.' " He spoke about the influence of the prayers of his second wife, the former Pauline van der Voort Rogers. In 1958, when David Wilkerson first went to Brooklyn to begin Teen Challenge, she was immediately involved in supporting the work. It was natural, then, that Wilkerson and John Benton, now director of the Walter Hoving Home, came to Hoving for financial help. Hoving was able to refer them to a foundation which granted funds to Teen Challenge.

Mrs. Hoving died in 1976. In the fall of 1977 Hoving married Jane Pickens Langley in New York City. He and his first wife, Mary Osgood Field, were divorced in 1936. In addition to their daughter Petie, they had a son Thomas who was the director of the Metropolitan Museum of Art.

BIBLE AS SOURCE OF SPIRITUAL INSIGHT

Besides prayer, Hoving turns to the Bible as a source of spiritual insight and strength. He reads the New Testament every evening, he says, and has gone through it dozens of times. Other reading materials that Hoving has found especially helpful include *Guideposts,* the monthly inspirational magazine, and books by the best-selling author Hal Lindsey, who writes about prophecy and the soon return of Jesus Christ.

Hoving also believes a Christian's relationship to a church is very necessary. But, he added quickly, "More churches should talk about a personal relationship to Jesus. People are hungry to be told the simple truth."

When asked one of the concluding questions I used in most of the interviews for this book, "Should a Christian expect to be sitting on top of the world all the time?" Hoving almost snorted.

"A person who thinks *that* isn't very smart," he declared. He went on to tell how some adversities in his life were used by God: "He makes life difficult for us, for that's how we grow. It's like exercise for a baby."

Walter's first job, when he was fresh out of Brown University in 1920, was in the filing department of a large insurance company.

"It was a block square, with files all over," Hoving recalled. "I made a map of the place and had a plan to put the file clerks on roller skates. Then it could have been run with half the staff."

But instead of taking kindly to his suggestion, Hoving's bosses fired him for the idea.

Hoving early earned a reputation for having a mind of his own, even a stubborn streak, though such episodes as his firing tested him and helped him grow, he says.

His second job was payroll clerk in an auto repair shop. Pay was a miserable four to five dollars a week for the staff. It wasn't long before he latched onto a higher-paying job. But just before he quit, without authority he raised the salaries of everyone in the shop.

Hoving also remembers two bosses, one at Montgomery Ward's and the other an official of Genesco, who were very difficult to work under.

"But this was good for me," he conceded. "The Lord wanted me to have a little suffering—I needed it."

Summing up his philosophy of hard work as making the best use of God-given abilities and being open to a personal relationship with God, Hoving eased back in his chair and looked out across one of the sales floors where he daily mingles with customers and his sales force of 750 persons:

He continued, "I think the Lord can use you where you can best be used if you really let Him in and if you are where your own proclivities, abilities, and aptitudes fit in. That's certainly true in my case.

"A Christian shouldn't expect to sit on top of the world all the time. But you can do very constructive work if you depend on the Lord. It's all very simple to me: God thinks in very simple terms."

As simple as a plainly styled but beautifully crafted pin with only two words: TRY GOD.

*Frederick W.
and Ruth P. Cropp*

10

Pastoral Partners

On May 15, 1977, Frederick W. Cropp, a retired United Presbyterian pastor, and his wife, Ruth, were summing up the long years of fruitful service they had shared in God's ministry.

"I think we've been through it all—with people, with our loved ones, our children, ourselves," Fred said. "We've known financial ups and downs, troubles and deaths within the family. We've learned how to suffer with our own parents. Even the deaths and tragedies in our lives have given us strength.

"No one has had more fun in life than Ruth and I have. We've had hilarious times. A sense of humor has permeated the whole thing.

"Paul said what I hope I can say, 'I have fought the good fight, I have finished the course, I have kept the faith.' "

Just before Christmas, Fred died of a sudden heart attack, the fifth in recent years. The San Marino Community Church in California, where he served as pastor from 1952

118

through 1966, was packed for his memorial service.

The Reverend Rick Thyne, present pastor of the prestigious church, assured the mourners that Fred had, indeed, finished his course with honor and kept the faith.

"When we think of him, we don't think of how he died, but of how he lived. And oh, how he lived!" said Thyne. He went on to describe Cropp, who distinguished himself in World War II service as a military chaplain, and who was general secretary of the American Bible Society from 1939 to 1956. "He was a genuine, thoughtful, sensitive person who knew us and took time for us," Thyne said.

Fred was well suited to be a pastor, though he only served one other church besides the one in San Marino: historic First Presbyterian Church of Wheeling, West Virginia.

"He turned pastoral calls into an art form," observed Thyne. And his little notes and brief letters, which he always penned in turquoise ink, came to be treasured by their many recipients as vessels of wisdom, information and, at times, not too gentle reminders.

Fred, who sent clippings and notes from his files far and near, never did learn the difference between an envelope and a wastebasket, according to his son, Fred III. Thyne mentioned that fact during the funeral service, causing subdued chuckles to ripple through the pews.

It was *that* kind of memorial service—one which Fred Cropp would have enjoyed. In fact, he had planned the selection of hymns and passages of Scriptures emphasizing the triumphant hope and joy of the Resurrection.

Those who knew Fred and know Ruth think of them for how they lived.

While both of them were living in the Samarkand retirement center in Santa Barbara, California, I spent several afternoons allowing them to distill the essence of nearly fifty years as a husband-and-wife ministry team. Truly, as Pastor Thyne said at Fred's memorial service,

"Fred and Ruth were almost one hyphenated word, not lost in each other, but found there, in a shared ministry."

Fred, a native of a little coal and steel town in Ohio, was the son of a Presbyterian elder. A graduate of the College of Wooster and Princeton Theological Seminary, he was ordained in 1929 and later received honorary degrees from three colleges.

Ruth Perkins, a native Georgian and daughter of a Presbyterian pastor, taught high-school English literature in New York state before she and Fred were married. They met at the College of Wooster, where Ruth also was graduated.

Both sets of parents were Christian. When Fred and Ruth were about age twelve, they each respectively joined the church. Their childhood and student days were free of notable crises.

DIFFICULT EVENTS

"The first traumatic twenty-four hours I ever spent," recalled Fred, "was at the birth of our first son" (Frederick W. Cropp, III, now professor of geology at the College of Wooster). It was a difficult delivery. "The only time that I could pinpoint a direct word from God came then," said Fred. "I heard the Lord speak to me. He said, 'Frederick, it will be all right!' "

It was Ruth's turn to respond to my initial interview question: Once you became a Christian, what were the most trying or difficult events in your life?

She singled out five, three involving the deaths of close loved ones.

The first crisis, she said, was when she and Fred were forced to be apart during the four war years he served as military chaplain of III Corps in Europe. She had the care of their two small sons Fred III and Robert.

A spiritual resource that Ruth and Fred had developed

at the very outset of their marriage served her in good stead during those single-parent days.

"The fact that we established our family altar, our devotional period together, at the beginning of our married life was preventive maintenance," Ruth explained. "It was building us up and giving us strength to meet the things that were ahead of us. It was a special part of our daily schedule. Of course, it never occurred to us that we were going to have trials and tribulations."

When Fred was away, Ruth and Fred read the same passages in the New Testament on the same day. "I didn't feel I could begin the day without reading the Word," said Ruth. Every day, twice a day, Ruth read the Bible and a devotional thought to the boys and prayed with them.

Later, Ruth was selected as one of fifteen parents from the White Plains, New York, Parent-Teacher Association to be interviewed for a magazine article.

"How did you get through all of that?" asked the interviewer when Ruth told her about her experiences with the boys during the war.

"I couldn't have gotten through it if I hadn't gotten down on my knees at night and asked the Lord to forgive me for all the mistakes I'd made with the children," Ruth replied. "Then, before I got out of bed in the morning, I asked Him to help me through all of those problems."

The reporter put down her pencil and looked up at Ruth. "Do you believe all that?"

"Of course I do."

STRENGTH AND GUIDANCE FROM THE LORD

For the next few minutes Ruth found herself witnessing to the young reporter and counseling her. Ruth told how much her faith meant to her, and how the Lord had strengthened her and given guidance through prayer.

While Ruth was coping with the children stateside, Fred was overseas giving spiritual counsel to GIs. He received the Bronze Star decoration and the Commendation Ribbon and became vice-president of the Military Chaplains' Association.

In 1943, during the Battle of the Bulge, there was grim going for Fred, whose unit was under fire.

"I was a chaplain, of course," Fred began, as if he were telling a war story (which, in a way he was) and I was supposed to be dishing out this stuff. I felt I had to at least keep ahead of the troops on the inner braces of life."

Fred did. A major source of inspiration, which he passed on to his men, was the devotional book *Five Minutes a Day* by Robert E. Speer, the late secretary of the Board of Foreign Missions of the Presbyterian Church. The book, reprinted in paperback, fall 1977, by Westminster Press was a classic in its day and was handed out to all United States military chaplains.

At the time Fred was serving in the European theatre, Ruth's younger brother, James H. Perkins, was a chaplain in Guam. He contracted a disease there and died a lingering death at forty-two, though he came back to the states and held a pastorate. He continued preaching, though he grew weaker, until he finally went to the hospital for six weeks.

But he got up and left the hospital on Easter morning to preach his sermon, "The Glory of the Resurrection." After the service he returned to the hospital and slipped into a coma from which he only temporarily recovered two days before his death.

"Each of us had a few minutes with him then and he was 'clear as a bell,' " Ruth recalled gratefully. "To see him face death like that was strengthening to us."

Interjected Fred: "When you go into a sick room, you get more help than you give, many times."

Another heartache for Fred and Ruth was the slow death by cancer of their daughter-in-law, Helen, Fred III's wife. The mother of four young children, Helen died gallantly. According to the Cropps, "The nurses told us she taught *them* how to live and die."

The third loved one whose death Ruth considered a difficult time was her beloved mother, Mrs. Frederick (Bertie Carol) Perkins, who lived for years with Fred and Ruth in San Marino. Though she had been delirious until just before she died, Mrs. Perkins passed on peacefully at age eighty-one.

FACING DEATH

The Cropps feel most Christians are not prepared to face the reality of death. Rather, they tend to avoid it by blocking it out.

"They deny it," said Fred. "Then life caves in on them and they are caught without any preparation at all. They wonder, 'Why has the Lord done this to me?' when the Lord hasn't done it at all. They should have been taught to pray that the Lord would give them strength to go through whatever lay ahead of them."

Not that Fred disparaged seeking help even in the eleventh hour of need. At another time, he said:

"When life tumbles in, people want a human voice to speak to them, a human ear to listen to their troubles. They need to know that the pastor himself, and his wife, are persons who, in confidence hear them, and hear them out, and know what they are up against and can help them.

"Call your minister when you have need; he'll come out even if it interferes with home life, if it's a real need."

The Cropps, no strangers to suffering, have devoted much thought and prayer to its meaning and mystery.

"But why does God send this to me?" Fred once wrote in the bulletin of the San Marino Community Church.

"If God is good why does He let this happen to anyone?"

"Look what God has done to me!

"In the wake of every personal or group tragedy, these are the words which come quickly to our minds and as quickly to our lips.

"What is the best thing to say?

"We are not willing to accept John Calvin's observation that God's will is so far above man's ability to understand that it is inscrutable. We want a better answer than that.

"The least 'dusty answer' I know is based on what a famous English preacher of 100 years ago said. Frederick W. Robertson observed that there are three principles at work in weaving the warp and woof of our lives. They are apparently incompatible and self-contradictory, yet we observe and believe that all three are at work."

ANSWERS

"The first is that 'there is a Divinity that shapes our ends, rough-hew them how we will.' God *is* sovereign and God is good, and we are in the hands of the Father who not only cares but has a plan for our lives," Fred continued.

"The second principle is that our fate is in our own hands. We do decide which way our souls go and our blessedness and our misery are the results of our own choices and our actions.

"The third principle is that there are accidents. 'Time and chance happeneth to them all.'

"The next time you question, look at these three elemental principles. Which one can you see most clearly? Are not the other two involved?

"Then—and this is most important of all—what is your reaction? What are you going to do about it? Where do you go from here?

"The problem has baffled everyone. The answering reaction of a Christian calls for trust and heroism."

Fred himself was forced to ask why. Several years later

when he suffered the first of a series of heart attacks that mandated a much restricted schedule and diet. That was a crisis both for Fred, who had to give up preaching, because of stress, and for Ruth, who sat beside him during each heart attack.

"It was a traumatic thing to give up preaching—it was a part of my life," admitted Fred, but without complaint. "The Lord gave us grace to live with the heart attacks—and through them all fear of death is gone."

Fred was ready, then, when his appointment with the last enemy came early on the morning of December 22 1977. Ruth rode with him in the ambulance to the hospital, where he expired.

Never too old to find and apply new truth, Fred characteristically followed up our interview with a note in turquoise ink and a clipping from the *London Times*. Fred commented that in the article he had discovered a new word—*orthopraxy*.

"Orthopraxy (right-acting)," said the article, is just as important as orthodoxy (right-thinking); and is indeed a condition of it."

"Orthopraxy," wrote Fred, "joined with orthodoxy, makes for a good life in the Spirit. Ruth and I have been trying to say that our life's goal has been a wedding of these two."

Beyond doubt, Ruth and Fred were adept at combining right thinking and right acting in the Spirit because they drew so heavily from the whole arsenal of available spiritual resources.

THE THINGS THAT HELP

First and foremost, they listed the Scriptures—unadorned. That means straight Bible reading, Fred explained, adding, however, that the reading of new versions and translations brings new light to the Old Word. "The Scriptures have answers to every crisis and problem that occurs," said Fred, the one-time Bible society secretary.

Commentaries and devotional literature also are useful, the Cropps said. Volumes of such material fill whole shelves in the Cropp apartment at Samarkand. Turning to a shelf of books by the British Methodist, Leslie Weatherhead, Fred told me how much they had meant to him, particularly his *House of Prayer.*

Fred said he had read John Baillie's classic, *Diary of Private Prayer,* once a year for twenty years. And he and Ruth read and reread David Mace's *Whom God Hath Joined.* Fred gave copies to couples whom he married.

Fred also turned frequently to the great poets Browning and Milton—"They have always fed me."

Other favorites include the works of mystic Evelyn Underhill, psychiatrist Paul Tournier, British apologist C. S. Lewis, Scottish Bible commentator William Barclay, and William Saroyan, known for penning, "Tomorrow we will make strength out of this sorrow."

Ruth added *These Days,* a Presbyterian daily devotional guide, and *Covenant Companion,* a paper put out by the Evangelical Covenant Church. She also reads *Christian Herald, A.D.,* and *Presbyterian Outlook.*

But the most help to her, other than the Bible, is Weatherhead's paperback *The Will of God.*

For decades, the Cropps followed the practice of rising before 7 A.M. in order to have devotions together before breakfast. "We got our marching orders for the day," said Ruth. "We used the Presbyterian *Mission Yearbook of Prayer* so that our hearts and minds and eyes were on the entire world before we had breakfast."

Another valued source of strength and help to the Cropps: the fellowship of other Christians and fellow ministers and their wives. A minister's life can be lonely even though he's almost constantly with people, Fred pointed out.

Ruth and Fred also felt strongly that public worship is an important resource for the Christian, in good times and bad.

"There's something in every service that gets to me," said Fred. "It may be the hymns, Scripture, or the architecture of the church. Regularity in worship is so necessary. It's a discipline—a self-discipline we can't force on people."

Closely allied to worship is praise—"practicing the presence of God."

"Praise," according to Ruth, "means getting up in the morning asking for strength from on high." But, she cautioned, "Don't say, 'Praise the Lord!' when you're struck down. Don't praise Him for that. Pray, thanking Him for His presence and help in the midst of the problem. That's how you praise God!"

"Christians get mugged and beaten," added Fred. "Paul was fighting the battle all his life. But he fought the fight and kept the faith. We've lived joyous lives with a sense of humor and adventure."

To Fred and Ruth, that's part of praise—to realize that life isn't funny, but that you can bear it if you have the gift of Christian good humor and laughter.

TITHING

Although it may seem paradoxical to consider tithing a *resource* for Christians, overcomers like the Cropps find it so.

Both Fred and Ruth were reared in poor homes, but they always tithed. And for many years of their ministry, they said they *over*-tithed.

During Depression days, Fred confided, scraping up the first 10 percent was jolly difficult. In fact, they often had to borrow from the Lord's money during months that had thirty-one days. When that happened, they would simply write out an *I. O. Thee* to God until they could pay it back.

Fred warned that they were not advocating tithing because it makes you rich. "A fallacy," he said, "is the thinking of quid pro quo Christians—those who figure that if you do this, you'll get that."

Rather, to the Cropps, though tithing may bring financial blessings, the real benefit is the harvest of joy and the sense of worth that comes from being partners with God and ministering to His people.

Speaking of storing up resources, the Cropps lamented that many of their contemporaries had not deposited too much faith or church relatedness.

This, they warned, leads to spiritual poverty and emptiness: "It's like a bank; you have to make deposits to build up interest."

Expounded Fred: "So many answers are not 'instant'; you just seldom get stabs of revelation if you haven't practiced the presence of God. It's never too late—but you have to take a kind of crash course in spiritual things—bone up for finals—if you haven't been making deposits regularly."

Using another analogy, Fred spoke about the Bible story in which a cast-out unclean spirit takes seven other spirits and enters into an empty man (*see* Matthew 12:43–45). "A vacuum may occur at the very point of conversion," Fred interpreted. "Christ theoretically fills a heart and life—and He does. But you need to entertain Him every day—otherwise He is gone.

"It's like coming to a deep well, but you have nothing to draw with. The Christian life is a process as well as an experience—and it continues."

Fred said he was a steady person and that it was not usual for him to have peaks and valleys in his spiritual pilgrimage. Ruth related that she was more apt to have what she called *concerns*. Asked to elaborate, she said,

"You know, the intuitive feelings of a mother—the need for assurance that all is well."

Fred broke in that he could always tell when Ruth was *concerned*, because she knelt longer in prayer that night.

Surprised to know that he was sensitive to that, Ruth rejoined: "After casting my burdens on the Lord I can get in bed and go to sleep. That may sound simplistic, but it's worked for me all these years."

OUT OF THE DAILY DOLDRUMS

When daily doldrums do encroach upon the Cropps' tranquility and inner peace, there's nothing like doing something to help someone else to lift them out of depression, they found.

"In helping others through their problems, my anxieties have disappeared," remarked Ruth. "Or put them in focus or perspective," inserted Fred.

Another way to overcome depression is to wait and listen instead of talk, the Cropps suggested. "Watch Christ in prayer and imitate Him."

While Fred and Ruth said they did not think it would be necessary for those reading this book to have had the same experiences they did in order to benefit from the spiritual lessons they learned, they did say that example and experience are good teachers.

"After experiencing death in our own families, we did a better job of helping others with this experience," noted Fred. "Until you know that what you're talking about works, you don't see it from the same perspective or have the strength to work it out."

"You don't need to have had the same experiences, but you need someone to help you deal with your difficulties," added Ruth.

The transference of Christian faith and the power of the Holy Spirit can take place by osmosis, according to Fred. "Seeing me calm in a threatening situation during the

war, men would ask, 'Chaplain, what have you got that I
haven't got?' I would try to tell them in a few words. My
testimony is for people to see how I'm living, though I
need to say it, too, in words."

As our second interview ended, Fred and Ruth showed
me a few of the many mementos grateful parishioners had
given them. There was a portrayal of the Lord's Supper
with brass figures from the choir. There also was a de-
coupaged, engraved Bible, open to 1 Corinthians 13,
Paul's famed passage on Christian love, from a youth.

"You have to have discipline all through your life,"
Ruth was saying, returning to a repeated theme. "Men-
tally, materially—first things first. The devotional life
first. I learned that lesson early in life when I was alone
without my sky pilot and I had to get my vitamins for the
day and give them to the boys, too."

"Eternity and the present life are all of one piece," Fred
summed up.

Seven months later Fred's words echoed in my mind as
I sat in the church where he had so often preached. This
time, it was Rick Thyne, paying final tribute to a great
man of the faith:

"Many of us believe in Christ, but few of us obey. Fred
believed in Jesus Christ—and obeyed Him, and loved
Him. He had an impact on many lives because of that.

"Oh, how he lived. He took every gift of God and lived
it all the way out to the edges.

"We give him back to You, O God—with significant
reluctance."

Joanne Cash Yates

Southern Singer

The pilot struggled to keep control of the rented six-seater Cherokee airplane as rain, hail, and wind battered the small craft. It was late October 1970 and the plane had unexpectedly veered into the path of a horrible storm.

Darkness closed in. Joanne Cash (later Yates) despaired for her life, though she knew the plane was being flown by an experienced pilot.

"I realized suddenly that I had been enclosed about by the hand of God," she said, recalling the frightening experience. "It was the third time I had been close to death's door." (The two previous times she had accidentally overdosed on drugs.)

As she clutched her seat in the storm-tossed plane, her life sped before her mind in quick review. She remembered all the times she had rejected Jesus Christ. The many times she had held on to the backs of pews in church—just as she was now desperately clinging to the seat in the Cherokee—saying no to God, refusing to walk down the aisle to receive salvation.

131

It had seemed as if she had always been searching for Jesus, but never found Him. Or, more accurately, had never been fully willing to let Him find her and take control of her life. Once she had walked forward to the altar of a church, but she was only nine years old at the time and was too young to understand what the preacher's invitation was all about.

And, though Joanne had been brought up in a Christian family of seven children, including her famous brother Johnny, in her teen years she had become convinced God didn't love her.

SALVATION IS . . . .

"I thought I had to be good; I didn't know salvation is believing in the Word of God," Joanne could say years later.

Now, at age thirty-two, her life was about to end, she thought, as the light plane groaned under the raging fury of the storm. She was sure they would all be killed.

Still, though she thought she "would go into eternity any moment and had bypassed His grace," Joanne uttered a silent, sincere prayer: "Have mercy, Lord, and let me live.

"I made all kinds of promises and meant them," Joanne recalled almost seven years later as we talked at the Nashville airport. "I promised God I would give Him all the rest of the days of my life."

About twenty minutes after her prayer, the hail stopped. Soon the little plane was more stable. It passed through the heavy rain and then crossed the line out of the clouds into sunshine.

The next Sunday Joanne went to Evangel Temple in Nashville. She sat in the second row.

God spoke, she says, reminding her what she had promised when her life had been endangered. But fear gripped her. She thought of the time when she was nine and went forward and nothing happened. Would it be an anticlimax like that again?

"But I went forward to the altar," Joanne related in her Southern-style drawl, "and I hollered out, 'Jesus, save me! Hurry up! I don't feel it yet.' "

She soon did.

Singer Connie Smith, a member of the church, had been praying for Joanne. Now she was kneeling beside her at the altar. And Jimmy Snow, pastor of the famed Pentecostal church and son of the country-western singer, Hank Snow, led her through to Christ.

"I prayed the sinner's prayer," Joanne said with a smile as we talked, her dark eyes dancing and her black hair tumbling out of a black and blue hat perched perkily on her head. "I asked Jesus into my heart. I believed it, made confession of my sins, and then thanked Him."

In His mercy, Joanne continued, God blessed her and lifted away all of her past, replacing it with a new beginning.

"I literally felt the drugs, sins, depression, and so much feeling of the past lifted off me. It was as if it came from my toes and gradually came upward. It was like black uncovering white. It was like 10,000 light bulbs just beginning to flash on. I felt clean and assured. There was not a doubt in my mind that I was saved. It was like for all the Christmases of my life I had never gotten a single present and now I was getting them all at once. It was beautiful!

"God really proved Himself to me. I had been a skeptic. I had been doubtful, stubborn, and so full of fear. One of the things the Lord did was to deliver all that fear from me. For, you see, you can't have fear *and* faith, and my heart was full of faith."

THE CASH FAMILY

The Cashes had always been a family of faith, Joanne remembers, but somehow early in her life fear had replaced faith in her heart. Only when the storm of her life and a stormy sky buffeting a small plane converged, was she willing to let Jesus Christ become the true captain of her soul.

Joanne, born March 9, 1938, was next to the baby among the seven children born to Ray and Carrie Cash in Dyess, Arkansas. Singer Tommy Cash is the youngest. Jack, the only one not living, was killed in 1944.

Johnny Cash's songs about cotton farming and hard times are not plucked out of his imagination. The Cashes farmed forty acres of cotton. But, though money was not plentiful, "my daddy was such a good provider," Joanne remembers, "that the family was never in serious need."

When Joanne was sixteen, the family moved from the farm into the town of Dyess, where Joanne attended high school. The night she was graduated, she boarded a plane for Nuremberg, Germany, to join the young Army enlisted man she had married in 1955. She was seventeen.

Two years later she returned to the United States. After nine more years the marriage ended in a divorce which left her alone with three children, Charlotte, Jeff, and Rhonda.

She had soon realized the marriage was, to use her words, "wrong and bad—I was a young, inexperienced, unsaved teenager."

Yet, through all of this, Joanne had always thought that the "most wonderful thing anyone could ever be was a Christian. It had been one of my life's ambitions to be a Christian and marry a preacher."

At the same time, Joanne had grown up seeing people all around her getting saved. Somehow, in her desperate search to find Christ, she had been like a person sitting hour after hour in a bus station, seeing everyone else getting on buses and going somewhere while never leaving the waiting room herself.

By the time her marriage had gone sour and she had

health problems, Joanne was doubly convinced God didn't love her.

ADDICTION

When she developed a serious ear infection, she went to the Army base doctor in Germany. Telling him about her depression, she was assured that some pills would help her feel better.

"They made me feel terrific," she remembers all too well. "I was so naive; I didn't know what I was getting into. I didn't know about drugs."

Next she persuaded the doctor to furnish her with a two-month supply of uppers (dexedrine). All this time, she says, she was still searching for Jesus and for peace. But the pills provided an illusory, temporary—though immediate—sense of peace.

Soon she was addicted.

"Drugs and their abuse literally were created by Satan himself," Joanne believes. "Drugs will send you to hell—where I almost ended up."

The periods of divorce (she felt as if it was the only way out) and drug dependency were rough for Joanne, who feared God without knowing His care and purpose for her.

Feeling that "Jesus had turned His back on me," Joanne faced what she thought was a bleak future. She found a job in 1969 at a car rental counter in the Houston airport.

One day a phone call from her brother Johnny, followed by a letter, changed her direction in life.

"Johnny said point blank, right up front, 'You're on pills. I want you to put your things in a moving van and come home to Nashville and I want to help you 'cause I love you.' "

Joanne didn't argue. "John has always been a big protective brother to love and rescue me," Joanne said in tribute. "He's always willing, always there. If I'm down, discouraged, just a look, a pat on the back, an 'It's Ok, Baby,' is all it takes. He's so full of the Spirit of Jesus."

So Joanne came home to her family. John gave her a job at the House of Cash, the two-story white building with columns in Hendersonville that is Johnny's business office.

DOTTIE SNOW: ONE WHO HELPED

There, another Christian was to give Joanne a nudge towards the Lord who finally enfolded her a few months later in Evangel Temple.

Dottie Snow, wife of the church's pastor, was receptionist at the House of Cash. She witnessed, by her life and by her words, to Joanne. But it only made Joanne mad.

"I saw in Dottie everything I had ever wanted to be," Joanne explained. "I saw physical and spiritual beauty, cleanliness, joy, peace, and radiance. But the enemy, Satan, had blinded me for so many, many years that I said, 'That's not fair.' "

One time, when Dottie was witnessing to her, Joanne told her that she was convinced, because of her sins, that God couldn't love her.

"What makes you so special that God can't love you?" Dottie retorted, reminding Joanne how Jesus loved Peter, who denied even knowing the Lord. And Dottie kept inviting Joanne to attend church with her.

Though she knew "it was so very, very real," Joanne kept resisting the invitation—until that storm experience in the Cherokee nearly a year later.

HARRY

Evangel Temple is special to Joanne for another reason. There, she met Harry Yates, who was saved a few months before Joanne. Also divorced, Harry's circumstances were similar to Joanne's including having three children.

The friendship between Harry and Joanne blossomed when they went on a church trip to Israel in 1971.

"We literally fell in love in Tel Aviv," beamed Joanne as Harry, who had brought Joanne to our interview at the airport, nodded agreement. "Our romance, based on Christ's love, was good, right, clean, and pure," continued Joanne. "It was right out of a storybook." Three months later the pair was married in Evangel Temple, with all the Cashes looking on.

Harry, who had been Jimmy Snow's associate and principal of the church-related school at Evangel Temple for five years, is also a singer. The Yates Family, as they are called now, includes Harry and Joanne, Joanne's daughter Rhonda, who sings and plays the piano, and Candy Stevin, an older teenager from Mount Pleasant, Michigan. Harry mixes evangelistic sermons and counseling with the Yates Family singing and entertaining tours.

Joanne and Harry returned to Israel four times and have made numerous television appearances. Since their schedules have included more and more shows, they are on the road full time. The Yates sold their Nashville home in the summer of 1977 and moved into their thirty-foot motor home.

AIR-CONDITIONED MIRACLE

"You're sitting in one of our miracles right now," chuckled Joanne.

Indeed, I was sitting in the large swivel chair behind the wheel of the roomy machine, which was parked in the airport parking lot for our interview. I had flown in from New York that afternoon and was due in Louisville that night, so the airport rendezvous was practical and comfortable.

The air conditioner on top of the motor home hummed in the humid, 90-degree heat and I sipped a Pepsi, just removed from the motor home refrigerator. I, too, was happy to be sitting in one of God's air-conditioned miracles. How it happened was a story Joanne would come back to in a few minutes.

Right now, Joanne was telling where she turns for spiritual help in times of trouble since she turned her life over to Christ. And problems still come, she said, though they never overcome. Instead, she said with assurance, she and Harry are the overcomers, through the power of God's Word.

SOURCE OF STRENGTH THROUGH TRIALS

A verse Joanne says the Lord gave her when she knelt at the altar of Evangel Temple is: "Fear not, for I am with you. Do not be dismayed. I am your God. I will strengthen you; I will help you; I will uphold you with my victorious right hand" (Isaiah 41:10 LB).

"God's Word was my source of strength then and now," she elaborated. "Jimmy Snow told me that no matter what I went through, I should fear not. He showed me that God's right hand is Jesus. God has brought me through so many trials."

Describing a few of them, Joanne continued, "Trials can be a ladder to heaven. Climbing a ladder of trials and getting victory over them is like putting your treasures in a bank in heaven."

One of Joanne's heartaches has been the unhappy marriage of her daughter Charlotte, who, in July 1977, was twenty and divorced with a year-old baby.

"The thing that can hurt you the most as a parent is when your children are in trouble," declared Joanne, detailing how she and Harry had been helping Charlotte find a job and get readjusted as a single parent.

Saying that she had been in prayer often, Joanne indicated the experience had caused much discouragement and depression.

When beset with difficulties, Joanne takes her Bible and opens it to one of two favorite passages, either Isaiah 41:10 quoted above or: "And I have given you authority over all the power of the Enemy, and to walk among serpents and scorpions and to crush them. Nothing shall injure you!" (Luke 10:19 LB). These verses are marked, circled, and double circled in her Bible.

Putting her finger on the circled verse, Joanne prays: "You said it, Lord, and I'm taking You at Your Word. You promised me that nothing's going to hurt us.

"As I am saying this," she confided to me, "we are going through and *out* of a financial crisis."

The bills had stacked up, and the Yates wanted to make a clean start without debts when they went on the road full time with their traveling ministry.

For financial sufficiency, as in everything else, Joanne feels God's Word can be trusted: "I lift up God's Word and say, 'You promised to supply all our needs. And we firmly believe that.' God has never failed me, and He never will."

In an apt analogy, Joanne compared God's testing of our trust in Him to the home canning she often watched her mother do.

"When I was a child my mother would screw a lid so tight on a fruit jar when she was sealing it that it would hurt her hand. I feel sometimes when we're going through a trial that we're being squeezed so tight—right to the very, very breaking point—that we feel like we're going to crack open and just explode and give up. But just before we break, God stops squeezing. And we say, 'Wow! Isn't it wonderful to be released!' "

And, according to Joanne, after each trial, the Christian can feel stronger in the Lord and more ready to trust Him the next time.

Ultimately, a believer reaches the point where he can praise God for his trials.

Even when one is downcast and needs to be shown

some light and encouragement, Joanne feels, he can take his needs before God in prayer. She and Harry often pray and talk to the Lord together, lightening the load and brightening the road, she said.

SHARING THE BURDEN

She also spoke of the uplift that comes from sharing burdens with closest friends. For the Yates, these include their pastor and his wife, Jim and Dottie Snow, brother Johnny Cash and his family, and Joanne's mother and father, who live in Hendersonville. The Yates also cherish the warmth and help available in small prayer groups.

How far a person should go in making specific needs and desires known to God was a question of considerable interest to me as Harry and Joanne and I talked about how they prayed for their motor home.

"It was all of God, not Johnny Cash," insisted Joanne, who, like the famed country superstar, often wears black just because she likes it.

BEING SPECIFIC WITH GOD

"I believe in being specific with God; He's a specific God," she added, noting that she and Harry felt called on the Fourth of July 1976 to go "full time on the road, totally on faith. So we had to be specific."

In the case of the motor home, as in other prayer requests, Joanne wrote on a pad of paper exactly what she wanted God to do. The list, she said, specified that it be an Executive Home, would have a microwave oven, a color TV, an eight-track stereo and cassette system, a refrigerator with an ample freezer, and a green interior.

"Wait a minute," I interrupted. "Even down to the inside color? Do you ask God what color dresses you should get, too?"

"It's important to God what color dress I get," Joanne replied. "If I ask for a blue dress, God will give me a blue dress."

"But what if He gives you another color?" I persisted.

"Well, He might think I look better in another color," Joanne smiled.

I glanced around, noting the green upholstery, microwave oven, and the sound system, just as she had outlined. I had no further questions.

"If I had asked for a 1961 Winnebago, that's exactly what we would have gotten," Joanne continued, picking up the thread of motor home conversation. "But we asked for the best—a new thirty-foot Executive Home. I was asking for the best because I'm the King's kid. A loving heavenly Father will give good gifts, both material and spiritual."

Once she has written out her prayer request, Joanne places the paper on top of her Bible. Then she lays her hands on the list-covered Bible and thanks God for answering the need.

In the case of the motor home, she and Harry "thanked God and believed we had already received it from God," she said. It works, she added, for anything a child of God needs.

Dell Robinson, a Southern California man, sold Harry and Joanne his nearly-new Executive Home at a substantially reduced price. It came, as he had originally ordered it, with the green interior and other specifications Joanne had asked for long before she had seen that particular motor home.

"Ask God for something once, specifically, from your heart" advised Joanne, "and then receive it from God. From that moment on, thank the Lord for it, as if you already have received it."

SOME SPIRITUAL LESSONS LEARNED

But expect testing between the time you make the prayer and the time the prayer is answered!

"I promise you," she challenged, "that before you get it, the devil will see to it that it seems impossible—it will look hopeless. But keep thanking God for having received it. This is your test of faith. 'Now faith is the substance of things hoped for, the evidence of things not seen' " (Hebrews 11:1 KJV).

Applying what she was preaching to the present, Joanne added that she believed a financial miracle was taking place at the very moment. "We believe and we receive that our bills are totally paid—I receive this as being done," she prayed.

"Take God at His Word," she said, looking up. "That's what it's all about. When we have done what we are humanly able to do in a situation, then God steps in. But He expects us to do all we can, too."

The victorious Christian is apt to have ups and downs, doubts and perplexities, despite the spiritual resources that are available, Joanne believes.

"Some say the believer is all smiles, joyful, and has no problems," she explained. "But we are still human as long as we're in this body. We're still prone to argue, fail, fall on our faces, and make mistakes. We still have a sinful nature.

"Christians who on the outside are so seemingly superspiritual haven't learned their wisdom yet—that sweet, deep wisdom that comes with the settling-down time," Joanne continued.

She said Christians need to learn how to use times of coming down from spiritual highs to let God teach wisdom and love. The times a follower of Christ falls and fails can be learning times, times to grow stronger in faith.

Sometimes, she conceded, she doesn't feel on cloud nine as she did when she went down the aisle in Evangel

Temple and hollered, "Jesus, save me!" That is all right, though.

"When that happens, you wonder if you're backsliding, and you ask, 'Do I have to put it on?' You're not backsliding; you're coming to the walking period in your life," she commented. "You've been crawling, now it's time to walk. Let God love you and teach you—even spank you if needed, as a good daddy spanks his baby because he loves him.

"I've gotten so many Holy Spirit spankings it's unreal," she laughed.

Joanne took a sip of coffee she had brewed in the plug-in coffee pot that runs off the 110-volt generator in their motor home.

"Yes," she answered to my final question, "Christians do worry. Worry is something humans face, but it never does any good."

Supremely, to Joanne Cash Yates, the Word of God is the place to go for every problem, every worry, whether it's physical, financial, or spiritual.

"You're still in this labor called life," she concluded, "and it's a testing time."

Paul S. Rees

12

Elder Statesman

"I can't remember a time when I wouldn't have considered myself a Christian of sorts," says Dr. Paul S. Rees, who has been called an elder statesman of the Christian faith.

Reared in a Christian home, this man of God, who is listed in *Who's Who in America,* was born in 1900 to a father who was a Quaker minister and a mother who was also a recorded minister in the Society of Friends.

Yet there came a definite time, when young Paul was a freshman at the University of Southern California, that he experienced what he calls his own assurance of salvation.

It was a very private affair, in the seclusion of his bedroom. But it was the beginning of a very public life that has spanned fifty years of active ministry as a pastor, ministerial superintendent, vice-president of the Evangelical Covenant Church of America, president of the National Association of Evangelicals, minister to ministers in Billy Graham Crusades, and vice-president and

144

editor-at-large for World Vision International, the Christian humanitarian agency.

It was also the starting point for a student who was a philosophy major and who became very good at putting his point across in words: Paul has written fourteen books, including *Don't Sleep Through the Revolution* and *Men of Action in the Book of Acts*. He is also the author of numerous pamphlets on stewardship, evangelism, and the Holy Spirit. Frequently in demand as a lecturer, he has conducted missionary and preaching rallies, often addresses college groups and commencement assemblies, has spoken in sixty countries and for eighteen years was a radio preacher.

But Paul Rees, a kindly, soft-spoken man who, one suspects, must be adored by his grandchildren, has weathered the storms of life. He has felt the sting of rebuke and rejection at the hand of a famous Christian leader and erstwhile friend. He has suffered through the critical illness and untimely death of a beloved brother. He has comforted his wife in the death of their infant son. And he has known the tension caused by closed banks and canceled engagements during the Great Depression.

But in all these, Paul is more than a conquerer—through Christ, his Lord.

CRISES OF FAITH

The first big trauma Paul remembers happened when he was seventeen years old—prior to his assurance of salvation experience at USC.

Paul's father, Seth, became involved, at that time, in what Paul calls "a deep and serious misunderstanding with other Christian leaders."

"I saw my father suffer," Paul said as we talked early one summer morning in Paul's motel room in Arcadia, a few blocks from his occasional office at World Vision headquarters in the Los Angeles suburb of Monrovia. "It made an impression on me so deep it was a crisis—an ordeal—in my own life."

Young Paul keenly felt the injustice in his father's experience. But there was something that made an impression, deeper even, than this profound trauma. It was the absence of bitterness in Seth Rees's spirit.

"The way in which my father prayed in his study and at our family altar set an example for me I've never forgotten," Paul said softly and evenly as the image of his father passed before his eyes. "It's an example for which I cannot but give thanks to God."

Paul added: "To witness the profound anguish of my father's spirit, but without bitterness or recrimination, was used by the Holy Spirit to give direction to my thinking about how a Christian should behave under provocation."

That memory of his father stood Paul in good stead thirty-seven years later.

But between the anguish of seeing his father's travail of soul and Paul's decision to prepare for the ministry came that bedroom experience when Paul was a freshman. Paul remembers being under the influence of a very strong, austere sermon he had heard on the doctrine of punishment for sin and the concept of hell as presented in the New Testament.

Paul admits fear was a motivating force in his decision to make sure his soul was right with the Lord. But he believes fear can be a legitimate means to lead people to a decisive act of choosing Christ. Yet, he would add immediately that the highest motive must be love. To him, the two seemed complementary rather than mutually exclusive. And so a decision of eternal destiny was made as he knelt alone in his room.

Close on the heels of that experience came a period of testing and turmoil about Paul's choice of a vocation. Paul's preferences, in order, were to be a lawyer or a college philosophy professor.

SIGNALS FROM THE HOLY SPIRIT

But Paul kept getting signals from the Holy Spirit to go into the ministry. He described the resolution of the dilemma this way:

"When that came to a head, I had in a very quiet way an experience which went beyond merely my affirmation of what I now believe was God's call. It became what is variously described as the 'filling of the Spirit,' or 'full surrender,' or 'entire consecration.' "

Though Paul has had no experience of speaking in tongues, or glossolalia, it was to him a "total commitment, a deep feeling of reliance in the Holy Spirit—a very intimate sense of reliance."

About five years later, during a trip around the world in 1925 with his parents, sister, and younger brother, Paul faced what he calls another major test of his faith.

His brother Seth, Jr., who was sixteen at the time, became deathly ill in Japan with a severe case of small pox. Paul remembers his brother was broken out over his entire body.

Seth, Jr., was rushed to a small isolation center in Kobe, where he remained at death's door for days and days. Troubled by communications problems, the rest of the family, aliens in an alien land, were quartered in a nearby hotel. Their anguish was very intense, Paul vividly remembers, and they went to see his brother every day.

But because of the highly contagious nature of the disease, they were not allowed to enter the isolation center. They were required to stand back, in the open air, about twenty-five feet in front of the paperlike doors of the chamber where Seth, Jr., was confined.

One night, as Paul and his father, Seth, stood there, they were both sure Seth, Jr., was going to die. They left, sorrowfully, and Seth's body shook with sobs as he and Paul turned into the street to walk back to their hotel. In deep distress, Paul couldn't restrain his tears either. As father and son tried to console each other, Paul suddenly heard someone whistling in the dark of night. They could not see any trace of the whistler, and the tune was indeed unlikely in an out-of-the-way street in Kobe in 1925—"What a Friend We Have in Jesus."

Paul and his father in their moment of extreme distress were immediately strengthened and uplifted by that song in the night.

And it proved to be a turning point in Seth, Jr.'s illness. He recovered and made the trip back to America on the ship with his family.

In a twist of events that Paul cannot fully comprehend, his brother died the next year, however, when gangrene complications followed an emergency appendectomy.

But even in this unexpected loss after the earlier healing in Japan, God's comfort was near and real to the Rees family. "The outpouring of love, letters, and the assurance of prayers by friends made us feel the Christian community was a larger family than we had thought," Paul recalls.

The third major crisis of faith came to Paul in Pasadena, California, when his second child was born. Paul and Edith P. Brown had been married in 1926, and their first child, Evelyn Joy, was born the next year. But Paul, Jr., their first son, born in 1933, lived less than thirty-six hours.

Paul well remembers breaking the word to Edith that the infant had expired. As Paul held Edith's hand, he sat on the edge of her hospital bed and they read from the Bible together.

As he relived that moment, Paul told me, "I can see tears rolling down her cheeks—she was not distraught; it was a mingling of peace and pain. It was a totally new experience for me as a man and as a father. She didn't make a big point out of the word 'why?' It was there, but it didn't become a kind of challenge to the Lord's oversight of our lives."

The Reeses were blessed with two more children. Daniel Seth was born in 1935, and Julianna, in 1937.

MONEY IN SHORT SUPPLY

Though Paul and Edith can now afford two apartments, one in Boca Raton, Florida, where they spend the winters, and their summer apartment in Northbrook, Illinois, there were days during the Great Depression in the early 1930s when money was in very short supply.

At the time, Paul was engaged in itinerant evangelistic work, with Kansas City as home base. Offerings, Rees remembers, were very small. But that was all there was, and Paul and Edith were grateful for any money at all.

So, when a telegram came from northern New York where he was scheduled to preach a three-week crusade, canceling out at the last minute, Paul had reason to feel destitute. Time hung heavy, and there were bills to pay.

"For a few days I was depressed," Paul admitted.

But soon Paul remembered having spoken several years earlier at a church camp in Minnesota. The director, a Methodist pastor, had told Paul, "If you ever have a cancellation in your evangelism schedule, let me know."

Paul sent a telegram to the pastor of the Park Avenue Methodist Church in Minneapolis telling him that he did, indeed, have a cancellation. The dates were available, and the pastor asked Paul to preach in his church.

But Paul sees the evangelistic services as more than a way the Lord provided for the Rees's immediate financial needs. Some members of the First Covenant Church of Minneapolis were in the audience and were impressed with Paul's preaching.

They, too, stored up that knowledge for possible use later on. Several years later, when the church became immersed in problems of pastoral leadership, Rees was asked to supply the pulpit. He promised he could give them nine months of interim preaching.

It turned out to be twenty years, for he became pastor of the First Covenant Church of Minneapolis from 1938 to 1958.

Rees refers to that call that came to him as an example of the sufficiency God wants to give us when the going is tough.

"Jesus said, 'When the Holy Ghost comes, He will bring all things to your remembrance,' " Paul remembered. (*See* John 14:26 kjv.) He went on to note that Jesus was speaking to His disciples, but that the truth of the passage is nevertheless applicable to present-day persons and circumstances. "The Holy Ghost caused me to remember during the Depression what Dr. George Vallentyne, the Methodist minister in Minneapolis, had said to me about letting him know if I had a speaking cancellation," Paul explained.

The fifth major testing of Paul's faith came in 1954 at the time when he was minister to ministers for the Billy Graham Crusades in London as he had also served for Graham Crusades in Scotland and Australia.

A well-known fundamentalist leader who had known Paul's father turned on Paul in a series of letters and peppered him with allegations that if he had had the guts that his father had, he would denounce Billy Graham.

The attack was a painful experience for Paul.

But the memory of how his father had withstood criticism and unwarranted hostility without rancor or retaliation was a soothing balm. "I was able to pray in love for my accuser," Rees said simply.

RESOURCES AVAILABLE TO CHRISTIANS

Continuing our conversation in Rees's motel room as he began preparing for a 7:30 A.M. breakfast meeting, Paul spoke of some of the resources available to Christians in time of testing and crisis.

"It troubles me a bit that so many books and articles tend to minimize and underplay the emphasis on God's adequacy for tough testing times," he declared.

"There are resources—God is able to make all grace abound."

On the other hand, Rees stressed that, though the Christian shouldn't lose sight of what the grace of God can do, neither should he be unrealistic. "We are not living in a perpetual bubble bath of good feelings," he said, adding: "Yet, even when I'm conscious of having let the Lord down, there is always the feeling that this wasn't fate. There could have been a better reaction on my part than that."

To Rees, the concept of the victorious Christian life is not a neurotic emotionalism— a continual feeling of one's spiritual pulse, a nervous attempt to discover whether one has fallen below a self-set standard. Rather, the answer for the Christian is to keep immersing himself in the Scriptures. For, as he does that, Rees believes, he will keep discovering new insights and God's Word will become personally relevant, both for correction and for support.

Another resource called forth by Rees is an ongoing conversation between the Christian and the Holy Spirit. Frank Laubach of the World Literacy Crusade is Paul's model for this: "This naturalness with which this man conversed with the Holy Spirit is so down-to-earth. It's not eerie, weird, or put-on."

In his later years, Rees has become growingly dependent on the Christian community as a source of spiritual strength and help for day-to-day living.

Despite the disappointment of seeing his father embroiled in serious conflict with Christian leaders, and despite his own conflict with one, Paul was able to say with joy: "The closeness of my relationship to Christians I know well and who know me well has become a priceless thing. It provides a kind of base for strength to know that people really mean it when they say, 'There isn't a day that I don't pray for you.'

"This has a dual effect: It generates strength in me and it also makes me feel similarly responsible to pray for other members of the Christian community."

Paul, who celebrated with Edith their Golden Wedding anniversary in 1976, has now outlived all of those senior men of God who helped mold and mature him when he was a youthful preacher-in-the-making. He has outlived many of his peers and respected contemporaries. In light of a life spent serving Jesus Christ, Paul has distilled the essence of his strong and persistent convictions into ten points. These were reprinted in "Christian Education Trends," a monthly newsletter circulated privately to ministers and other Christian educators by the David C. Cook Publishing Co. in the spring of 1977:

1. I shall go to my grave affirming that Jesus Christ is what I mean by absolute reality. Not the church, which is less than eternal; not the Bible, which is instrumental rather than ultimate; but Jesus Christ, the Lord God revealed.

2. I shall go to my grave convinced that the church—the visible community of Christian faith and fellowship—needs to exhibit a unity that is perilously contradicted by the exclusive, self-defensive, and often warring divisions into which we have fractured and factioned ourselves. With time's passing, I am less and less impressed by our attempts to justify this rabbit-warren proliferation of our sects and subdivisions. Concurrently, I am increasingly struck by the flimsiness and self-serving of our arguments for going on as we are.

3. I shall go to my grave declaring that the human condition of estrangement from God is so profound that it can never be put right except as God in mercy

takes the initiative, as He has in Christ. At the Cross, the place of reconciliation has been found and founded, once-for-all and for all who will kneel to accept.

4. I shall go to my grave persuaded that rules and regulations for Christians, if used as means by which we pigeonhole our Christian comrades into "true" or "false," are legalistic devices for producing "cult" or "culture" Christianity instead of the Beloved Community of the New Testament.

5. I shall go to my grave firm in the feeling that one of the most frequent undetected sins of Christians is idolatry. Customs, tradition, forms, ideologies, organizations, institutions (including the State), precedents, structures, titles, clichés—in every one of them there is a potential idol. They arose, it well may be, out of historical necessity. We cling to them, or kowtow to them, or somehow perpetuate them, out of lethargy, or bigotry, or stupidity, or vanity.

6. I shall go to my grave believing that the long years of controversial "pulling and hauling" over the personal gospel vs. the social gospel was a poignant mis-calculation. There was myopia on both sides. Now, thank God, the signs point to clearer understanding.

7. I shall go to my grave with the conviction that theological "tunnel vision" has kept multitudes of Christians, both clergy and laity, from discovering the wealth of Christlikeness that is open to them on the pages of the New Testament. A holiness of motivating love, offered both as gift and as growth, has been missed by masses of Christians. They have missed it because of their preoccupation with two-nature theories, or "after-all-I'm-only-human" rationalizations, or mistaken exegeses ("Paul saw himself a bigger sinner at the end than at the begin-

ning of his Christian life"), or justifiable fears of per-
fectionist excesses that they have witnessed or that
history has recorded. We are wrong, I am persuaded,
to set limits to what the grace of God can do in re-
deeming and refashioning the believing person.

8. I shall go to my grave asserting that nine-tenths
of our either-or's are abstractions of the mind rather
than reflections of reality. There are absolutes and
there is truth in situation ethics. There is subordina-
tion in family and other community life and there is
sexual equality. We do have a trustworthy Bible and
we do have a Bible whose authority is not derailed by
a misspelled word, or an erroneously translated term,
or an incorrect date.

9. I shall go to my grave believing that, side by
side with my ardent expectation of the Second Ad-
vent, most of our "signs of the times" sermons and
books are based on opportunism and a mistaken understanding of what the apocalyptic portions of Scripture are meant to teach us. These hot sermonic and
literary outpourings tend, in the cases of many Christians, to distract from the "occupy until I come"
mandate for missions and social responsibility.

10. I shall go to my grave unshakable in the faith-
confession that, all appearances to the contrary,
"Jesus is Lord."

> Thou, O Christ, art all I want.
> More than all in Thee I find;
> Raise the fallen, cheer the faint,
> Heal the sick and lead the blind.
>
> CHARLES WESLEY

Conclusion:
Through It All . . .

As I write this concluding chapter, I realize I was privileged to be the first person to hear the stories of these men and women in just the way they have been presented here. Their lives, and through them the power of God's Word and Holy Spirit, have been a blessing to me. I have been strengthened by just listening to these women and men of God.

Even as I was writing the various chapters, I found myself trying out some of the resources and techniques they suggested. I have deepened my resolve to let God's Word speak to me. I am seeking a more consistent prayer life. I am tasting anew the sustaining help and succor that comes from give-and-take relationships in a small corps of believers who are dedicated to each other—and to the Lord.

If you are like me, however, you didn't fully identify

with all the personalities in *The Overcomers,* but I hope you did find help from many. I suspect that if I had been able to assemble into the same room all fourteen persons interviewed, they wouldn't have seen eye to eye on all of the programs and methods for spiritual victories that were suggested. But, they *would* have spoken of the one Lord whom they had all seen through the eye of faith. One of the beautiful things in reviewing how God gave special resources to these men and women in *The Overcomers* is the rich diversity they represent—yet in a unity forged of one Spirit.

If you thought, when you began reading, that they were all cut out of the same material with a cookie cutter, you found out differently as you read chapter to chapter. Not only are their life stories utterly different, they also relate to the saving knowledge of Jesus Christ and the guidance of the Holy Spirit in thoroughly discrete ways.

Perhaps one man, woman, or couple will seem to you to be the most nearly ideal, a model for you to follow. Return to that chapter and reread it.

Perhaps Maria Von Trapp's method of deciding God's will—eliminating everything else and then doing the hardest thing which remains—speaks to you. Or—poles away—Joanne Cash Yates' writing out her request for a motor home, down to the last detail of interior color, placing the note on the Bible, and then thanking God for *already* providing it.

Don't let these apparent opposites distress you. If anything, the way different individuals respond to the molding, loving direction of God's will should confirm the validity of the Holy Spirit's leading.

Advice on specific courses of action may differ from Christian to Christian, but there is agreement on *where* to go to obtain that guidance. And the common thread through it all is that Jesus Christ is to be trusted, obeyed, and loved.

If I were to single out the most important spiritual lesson to be learned from these overcomers, it is the consistency of God—not the uniformity of God's servants. For God requires a right heart far more than He expects a *right* method.

In King David's famous Fifty-first Psalm (KJV), he contemplates giving God ritual sacrifice. But he concludes that that is not what God requires:

"For thou desirest not sacrifice; else would I give it: thou delightest not in burnt offering" (v. 16).

Rather, David rightly concludes, God is most concerned about his attitude: "The sacrifices of God are a broken spirit: a broken and a contrite heart, O God, thou wilt not despise" (v. 17).

The leaders who speak in *The Overcomers* are all submitting to the Lord, not looking for a universal blueprint from which all Christian lives are to be built, down to the last cross brace and door jamb.

All this is not to say there wasn't certain very basic agreement about what to do to get the victory when troubles mount, or how to cope with the vicissitudes when life gets "so daily." Turning to the Bible can bring the wisdom of God down to earth, they all said. Various forms of prayer and the counsel of wise, honest Christian friends were resources spoken of by almost all those interviewed. Some kind of worship experience in a body of believers, whether it is Catholic mass, Quaker silence, or altar-rail Pentecostal prayer, appeared to be "musts." A committed company in a smaller, more intimate fellowship also ranked high. Surprising—and pleasing—to me was the large percentage of overcomers who spoke of the help and inspiration they had received from great literature and the devotional classics, as well as contemporary works of Christian inspiration. Overcomers do read, and what they read helps!

Of course I am tempted to tack on my own ending to

this chapter, outlining where *I* turn for spiritual help in time of need, which is often. But I will resist that temptation head on, realizing that it would be both presumptuous and futile for me to improve upon what has already been said by those with more experience and authority. And, I have concluded, there is no neat formula that will work, plink-a-plink-a-plink, as Elisabeth Elliott would say.

But I do like Elton Trueblood's sensing God's presence *in the midst,* which fits in so nicely with E. V. Hill's glad news that he's never had to call an *emergency session* because he received directions from God in the very hour of his crises.

May His grace be sufficient for you and yours to overcome—through it all.